Selected Works
of
Edgar Allan Poe

Edited with Notes by Yoko Ikesue
Illustrated by Masaki Fujimoto

ASAHI PRESS

Selected Works of Edgar Allan Poe

表紙画 ： 藤本雅樹

Preface

Edgar Allan Poe (1809-49), a nineteenth-century American writer, has long been one of the most controversial and mysterious figures in world literature and his influence on specific genres in literature is unfathomable and immeasurable. He has achieved universal popularity in gothic fiction, contemporary cinema, and classical or popular music. According to successive recent discoveries of novel resources, his image has now been revisited and revised in some political, cultural, as well as biographical contexts.

Poe is taught in Japanese universities in three primary but often overlapping ways: as (1) a textbook in English language classes; (2) as materials for American cultural studies courses; and (3) as texts that require and sharpen critical intelligence in literature courses. Given the educational context of universities in Japan, improving English language skills is an important goal for these classes. Consequently, reading Poe is particularly appropriate, because added to the correctness of the grammar, the choice of words and phrases, and the composition of the stories, Poe provides an opportunity to master rhetoric. His works have classical and universal themes, such as death, love, revenge, and mourning, and show a variety of aspects of American culture. Musical pieces and movies influenced and inspired by Poe are also good materials for the understanding of his words and world.

Teaching Poe in Japan dates back to the Meiji era, during which Francis H. Underwood's *A Hand-Book of English Literature Intended for the Use of High Schools as well as the Companion and Guide for Private Students, and for General Readers, American Authors* (1875) was first used as the English textbook for the students of Kaisei Gakko (later, The University of Tokyo). After that, Patrick Lafcadio Hearn gave lectures at The University of Tokyo, and from the Taishō era to early Shōwa era Yonejiro Noguchi taught and studied Poe as an important figure of American literary history. Starting in the Meiji era many well-known writers and critics released translations of Poe's works. Since then his popularity among people of this country has continued to grow, and more than ten textbooks of his selected prose and poems have been published in the past fifty years.

I hope readers enjoy these stories and find much to ponder upon in every character on the following pages.

Finally, I wish to thank my friends, Mark Weisner, Robert Swier, and Preston Keido Houser, for help in many ways. Yoichiro Ogawa of Asahi Press has assisted the work on this textbook, and I am much in his debt.

YOKO IKESUE

September 2019

Contents

THE BLACK CAT

FOR the most wild, yet most homely narrative which I am about to pen, I neither expect nor solicit belief. Mad indeed would I be to expect it, in a case where my very senses reject their own evidence. Yet, mad am I not — and very surely do I not dream. But to-morrow I die, and to-day I would unburthen my soul. My immediate purpose is to place before the world, plainly, succinctly, and without comment, a series of mere household events. In their consequences, these events have terrified — have tortured — have destroyed me. Yet I will not attempt to expound them. To me, they have presented little but Horror — to many they will seem less terrible than *barroques*. Hereafter, perhaps, some intellect may be found which will reduce my phantasm to the common-place — some intellect more calm, more logical, and far less excitable than my own, which will perceive, in the circumstances I detail with awe, nothing more than an ordinary succession of very natural causes and effects.

From my infancy I was noted for the docility and humanity of my disposition. My tenderness of heart was even so conspicuous as to make me the jest of my companions. I was especially fond of animals, and was indulged by my parents with a great variety of pets. With these I spent most of my time, and never was so happy as when feeding and caressing them. This peculiarity of character grew with my growth, and, in my manhood, I derived from it one of my principal sources of pleasure. To those who have cherished an affection for a faithful and sagacious dog, I need hardly be at the trouble of explaining the nature or the intensity of the gratification thus derivable. There is something in the unselfish and self-sacrificing love of a brute, which goes directly to the heart of him who has had frequent occasion to test the paltry friendship and gossamer fidelity of mere *Man*.

I married early, and was happy to find in my wife a disposition not uncongenial with my own. Observing my partiality for domestic pets, she lost no opportunity of procuring those of the most agreeable kind. We had birds, gold-fish, a fine dog, rabbits, a small monkey, and *a cat*.

This latter was a remarkably large and beautiful animal, entirely black, and sagacious to an astonishing degree. In speaking of his intelligence, my wife, who at heart was not a little tinctured with superstition, made frequent allusion to the ancient popular notion, which regarded all black cats as witches in disguise. Not that she was ever *serious* upon this point — and I mention the matter at all for no better reason than that it happens, just now, to be remembered.

Pluto — this was the cat's name — was my favorite pet and playmate. I alone fed him, and he attended me wherever I went about the house. It was even with difficulty that I could prevent him from following me through the streets.

Our friendship lasted, in this manner, for several years, during which my general temperament and character — through the instrumentality of the Fiend Intemperance — had (I blush to confess it) experienced a radical alteration for the worse. I grew, day by day, more moody, more irritable, more regardless of the feelings of others. I suffered myself to use intemperate language to my wife. At length, I even offered her personal violence. My pets, of course, were made to feel the change in my disposition. I not only neglected, but ill-used them. For Pluto, however, I still retained sufficient regard to restrain me from maltreating him, as I made no scruple of maltreating the rabbits, the monkey, or even the dog, when by accident, or through affection, they came in my way. But my disease grew upon me — for what disease is like Alcohol! — and at length even Pluto, who was now becoming old, and consequently somewhat peevish — even Pluto began to experience the effects of my ill temper.

One night, returning home, much intoxicated, from one of my haunts about town, I fancied that the cat avoided my presence. I seized him; when, in his fright at my violence, he inflicted a slight wound upon my hand with his teeth. The fury of a demon instantly possessed me. I knew myself no longer. My original soul seemed, at once, to take its flight from my body; and a more than fiendish malevolence, gin-nurtured, thrilled every fibre of my frame. I took from my waistcoat-pocket a pen-knife, opened it, grasped the poor beast by the throat, and deliberately cut one of its eyes from the socket! I blush, I burn, I shudder, while I pen the damnable atrocity.

When reason returned with the morning — when I had slept off the fumes of the night's debauch — I experienced a sentiment half of horror, half of remorse, for the crime of which I had been guilty; but it was, at best, a feeble and equivocal feeling, and the soul remained untouched. I again plunged into excess, and soon drowned in wine all memory of the deed.

In the meantime the cat slowly recovered. The socket of the lost eye presented, it is true, a frightful appearance, but he no longer appeared to suffer any pain. He went about the house as usual, but, as might be expected, fled in extreme terror at my approach. I had so much of my old heart left, as to be at first grieved by this evident dislike on the part of a creature which had once so loved me. But this feeling soon gave place to irritation. And then came, as if to my final and irrevocable overthrow, the spirit of PERVERSENESS. Of this spirit philosophy takes no account.* Yet I am not more sure that my soul lives, than I am that perverseness is one of the primitive impulses of the human heart — one of the indivisible primary faculties, or sentiments, which give direction to the character of Man. Who has not, a hundred times, found himself committing a vile or a silly action, for no other reason than because he knows he should *not*? Have we not a perpetual inclination, in the teeth of our best judgment, to violate that which is *Law*, merely because we understand it to be such? This spirit of perverseness, I say, came to my final overthrow. It was this unfathomable longing of the soul *to vex itself* — to offer violence to its own nature — to do wrong for the wrong's sake only — that urged me to continue and finally to consummate the injury I had inflicted upon the unoffending brute. One morning, in cool blood, I slipped a noose about its neck and hung it to the limb of a tree; — hung it with the tears streaming from my eyes, and with the bitterest remorse at my heart; — hung it *because* I knew that it had loved me, and *because* I felt it had given me no reason of offence; — hung it *because* I knew that in so doing I was committing a sin — a deadly sin that would so jeopardize my immortal soul as to place it — if such a thing were possible — even beyond the reach of the infinite mercy of the Most Merciful and Most Terrible God.

On the night of the day on which this cruel deed was done, I was aroused from sleep by the cry of fire. The curtains of my bed were in flames. The whole house was blazing. It was with great difficulty that my wife, a servant, and myself, made our escape from the conflagration. The destruction was complete. My entire worldly wealth was swallowed up, and I resigned myself thenceforward to despair.

I am above the weakness of seeking to establish a sequence of cause and effect, between the disaster and the atrocity. But I am detailing a chain of facts — and wish not to leave even a possible link imperfect. On the day succeeding the fire, I visited the ruins. The walls, with one exception, had fallen in. This exception was found in a compartment wall, not very thick, which stood about the middle of the house, and against which had rested the head of my bed. The plastering had here, in great measure, resisted the action of the fire — a fact which I attributed to its having been recently spread. About this wall a dense crowd were collected, and many persons seemed to be examining a particular portion of it with very minute and eager attention. The words "strange!" "singular!" and other similar expressions, excited my curiosity. I approached and saw, as if graven in *bas relief* upon the white surface, the figure of a gigantic *cat*. The impression was given with an accuracy truly marvellous. There was a rope about the animal's neck.

When I first beheld this apparition — for I could scarcely regard it as less — my wonder and my terror were extreme. But at length reflection came to my aid. The cat, I remembered, had been hung in a garden adjacent to the house. Upon the alarm of fire, this garden had been immediately filled by the crowd — by some one of whom the animal must have been cut from the tree and thrown, through an open window, into my chamber. This had probably been done with the view of arousing me from sleep. The falling of other walls had compressed the victim of my cruelty into the substance of the freshly-spread plaster; the lime of which, with the flames, and the *ammonia* from the carcass, had then accomplished the portraiture as I saw it.

Although I thus readily accounted to my reason, if not altogether to my conscience, for the startling fact just detailed, it did not the less fail to make a deep impression upon my fancy. For months I could not rid myself of the phantasm of the cat; and, during this period, there came back into my spirit a half-sentiment that seemed, but was not, remorse. I went so far as to regret the loss of the animal, and to look about me, among the vile haunts which I now habitually frequented, for another pet of the same species, and of somewhat similar appearance, with which to supply its place.

One night as I sat, half stupified, in a den of more than infamy, my attention was suddenly drawn to some black object, reposing upon the head of one of the immense hogsheads of Gin, or of Rum, which constituted the chief furniture of the apartment. I had been looking steadily at the top of this hogshead for some minutes, and what now caused me surprise was the fact that I had not sooner perceived the object thereupon. I approached it, and touched it with my hand. It was a black cat — a very large one — fully as large as Pluto, and closely resembling him in every respect but one. Pluto had not a white hair upon any portion of his body; but this cat had a large, although indefinite splotch of white, covering nearly the whole region of the breast.

Upon my touching him, he immediately arose, purred loudly, rubbed against my hand, and appeared delighted with my notice.

This, then, was the very creature of which I was in search. I at once offered to purchase it of the landlord; but this person made no claim to it — knew nothing of it — had never seen it before.

I continued my caresses, and, when I prepared to go home, the animal evinced a disposition to accompany me. I permitted it to do so; occasionally stooping and patting it as I proceeded. When it reached the house it domesticated itself at once, and became immediately a great favorite with my wife.

For my own part, I soon found a dislike to it arising within me. This was just the reverse of what I had anticipated; but — I know not how or why it was — its evident fondness for myself rather disgusted and annoyed. By slow degrees, these feelings of disgust and annoyance rose into the bitterness of hatred. I avoided the creature; a certain sense of shame, and the remembrance of my former deed of cruelty, preventing me from physically abusing it. I did not, for some weeks, strike, or otherwise violently ill use it; but gradually — very gradually — I came to look upon it with unutterable loathing, and to flee silently from its odious presence, as from the breath of a pestilence.

What added, no doubt, to my hatred of the beast, was the discovery, on the morning after I brought it home, that, like Pluto, it also had been deprived of one of its eyes. This circumstance, however, only endeared it to my wife, who, as I have already said, possessed, in a high degree, that humanity of feeling which had once been my distinguishing trait, and the source of many of my simplest and purest pleasures.

With my aversion to this cat, however, its partiality for myself seemed to increase. It followed my footsteps with a pertinacity which it would be difficult to make the reader comprehend. Whenever I sat, it would crouch beneath my chair, or spring upon my knees, covering me with its loathsome caresses. If I arose to walk it would get between my feet and thus nearly throw me down, or, fastening its long and sharp claws in my dress, clamber, in this manner, to my breast. At such times, although I longed to destroy it with a blow, I was yet withheld from so doing, partly by a memory of my former crime, but chiefly — let me confess it at once — by absolute *dread* of the beast.

This dread was not exactly a dread of physical evil — and yet I should be at a loss how otherwise to define it. I am almost ashamed to own — yes, even in this felon's cell, I am almost ashamed to own — that the terror and horror with which the animal inspired me, had been heightened by one of the merest chimæras it would be possible to conceive. My wife had called my attention, more than once, to the character of the mark of white hair, of which I have spoken, and which constituted the sole visible difference between the strange beast and the one I had destroyed. The reader will remember that this mark, although large, had been originally very indefinite; but, by slow degrees — degrees nearly imperceptible, and which for a long time my Reason struggled to reject as fanciful — it had, at length, assumed a rigorous distinctness of outline. It was now the representation of an object that I shudder to name — and for this,

225 above all, I loathed, and dreaded, and would have rid myself of the monster *had I dared* — it was now, I say, the image of a hideous — of a ghastly thing — of the GALLOWS! — oh, mournful and terrible engine of Horror and of Crime — of Agony and of Death!

230 And now was I indeed wretched beyond the wretchedness of mere Humanity. And *a brute beast* — whose fellow I had contemptuously destroyed — *a brute beast* to work out for *me* — for me a man, fashioned in the image of the High God* — so much of insufferable wo! Alas! neither by day nor by night knew I

235 the blessing of Rest any more! During the former the creature left me no moment alone; and, in the latter, I started, hourly, from dreams of unutterable fear, to find the hot breath of *the thing* upon my face, and its vast weight — an incarnate Night-Mare that I had no power to shake off — incumbent eternally upon my

240 *heart!*

Beneath the pressure of torments such as these, the feeble remnant of the good within me succumbed. Evil thoughts became my sole intimates — the darkest and most evil of thoughts. The moodiness of my usual temper increased to hatred of all things

245 and of all mankind; while, from the sudden, frequent, and ungovernable outbursts of a fury to which I now blindly abandoned myself, my uncomplaining wife, alas! was the most usual and the

most patient of sufferers.

One day she accompanied me, upon some household errand, into the cellar of the old building which our poverty compelled us to inhabit. The cat followed me down the steep stairs, and, nearly throwing me headlong, exasperated me to madness. Uplifting an axe, and forgetting, in my wrath, the childish dread which had hitherto stayed my hand, I aimed a blow at the animal which, of course, would have proved instantly fatal had it descended as I wished. But this blow was arrested by the hand of my wife. Goaded, by the interference, into a rage more than demoniacal, I withdrew my arm from her grasp and buried the axe in her brain. She fell dead upon the spot, without a groan.

This hideous murder accomplished, I set myself forthwith, and with entire deliberation, to the task of concealing the body. I knew that I could not remove it from the house, either by day or by night, without the risk of being observed by the neighbors. Many projects entered my mind. At one period I thought of cutting the corpse into minute fragments, and destroying them by fire. At another, I resolved to dig a grave for it in the floor of the cellar. Again, I deliberated about casting it in the well in the yard — about packing it in a box, as if merchandize, with the usual arrangements, and so getting a porter to take it from the house. Finally I hit upon what I considered a far better expedient than either of these. I determined to wall it up in the cellar — as the monks of the middle ages are recorded to have walled up their victims.

275   For a purpose such as this the cellar was well adapted. Its walls were loosely constructed, and had lately been plastered throughout with a rough plaster, which the dampness of the atmosphere had prevented from hardening. Moreover, in one of the walls was a projection, caused by a false chimney, or fireplace, that had been
280 filled up, and made to resemble the rest of the cellar. I made no doubt that I could readily displace the bricks at this point, insert the corpse, and wall the whole up as before, so that no eye could detect any thing suspicious.

    And in this calculation I was not deceived. By means of a
285 crowbar I easily dislodged the bricks, and, having carefully deposited the body against the inner wall, I propped it in that position, while, with little trouble, I re-laid the whole structure as it originally stood. Having procured mortar, sand, and hair, with every possible precaution, I prepared a plaster which could
290 not be distinguished from the old, and with this I very carefully went over the new brickwork.* When I had finished, I felt satisfied that all was right. The wall did not present the slightest appearance of having been disturbed. The rubbish on the floor was picked up with the minutest care. I looked around
295 triumphantly, and said to myself — "Here at least, then, my labor has not been in vain."

    My next step was to look for the beast which had been the

cause of so much wretchedness; for I had, at length, firmly resolved to put it to death. Had I been able to meet with it, at the moment, there could have been no doubt of its fate; but it appeared that the crafty animal had been alarmed at the violence of my previous anger, and forebore to present itself in my present mood. It is impossible to describe, or to imagine, the deep, the blissful sense of relief which the absence of the detested creature occasioned in my bosom. It did not make its appearance during the night — and thus for one night at least, since its introduction into the house, I soundly and tranquilly slept; aye, *slept* even with the burden of murder upon my soul!

The second and the third day passed, and still my tormentor came not. Once again I breathed as a freeman. The monster, in terror, had fled the premises forever! I should behold it no more! My happiness was supreme! The guilt of my dark deed disturbed me but little. Some few inquiries had been made, but these had been readily answered. Even a search had been instituted — but of course nothing was to be discovered. I looked upon my future felicity as secured.

Upon the fourth day of the assassination, a party of the police came, very unexpectedly, into the house, and proceeded again to make rigorous investigation of the premises. Secure, however, in the inscrutability of my place of concealment, I felt no embarrassment whatever. The officers bade me accompany them in their search. They left no nook or corner unexplored. At length, for the third or fourth time, they descended into the cellar. I quivered not in a muscle. My heart beat calmly as that of one who slumbers in innocence. I walked the cellar from end to end. I folded my arms upon my bosom, and roamed easily to and fro. The police were thoroughly satisfied and prepared to depart. The glee at my heart was too strong to be restrained. I burned to say if but one word, by way of triumph, and to render doubly sure their assurance of my guiltlessness.

"Gentlemen," I said at last, as the party ascended the steps, "I delight to have allayed your suspicions. I wish you all health, and a little more courtesy. By the bye, gentlemen, this — this is a very well constructed house." [In the rabid desire to say something easily, I scarcely knew what I uttered at all.] — "I may say an *excellently* well constructed house. These walls — are you going, gentlemen? — these walls are solidly put together;" and here, through the mere phrenzy of bravado, I rapped heavily, with a cane which I held in my hand, upon that very portion of the brick-work behind which stood the corpse of the wife of my bosom.*

But may God shield and deliver me from the fangs of the Arch-Fiend! No sooner had the reverberation of my blows sunk into silence, than I was answered by a voice from within the tomb! — by a cry, at first muffled and broken, like the sobbing of a child, and then quickly swelling into one long, loud, and continuous scream, utterly anomalous and inhuman — a howl — a wailing shriek, half of horror and half of triumph, such as might have arisen only out of hell, conjointly from the throats of the damned in their agony and of the demons that exult in the damnation. 350

Of my own thoughts it is folly to speak. Swooning, I staggered to the opposite wall. For one instant the party upon the stairs remained motionless, through extremity of terror and of awe. In the next, a dozen stout arms were toiling at the wall. It fell bodily. The corpse, already greatly decayed and clotted with 355 gore, stood erect before the eyes of the spectators. Upon its head, with red extended mouth and solitary eye of fire, sat the hideous beast whose craft had seduced me into murder, and whose informing voice had consigned me to the hangman. I had walled the monster up within the tomb! 360

SHADOW — A PARABLE

Yea! though I walk through the valley of the *Shadow :*

— Psalm of David

Ye who read are still among the living; but I who write shall
have long since gone my way into the region of shadows. For
indeed strange things shall happen, and secret things be known,
and many centuries shall pass away, ere these memorials be
seen of men. And, when seen, there will be some to disbelieve,
and some to doubt, and yet a few who will find much to ponder
upon in the characters here graven with a stylus of iron.

The year had been a year of terror, and of feelings more intense
than terror for which there is no name upon the earth. For many
prodigies and signs had taken place, and far and wide, over sea
and land, the black wings of the Pestilence were spread abroad.*
To those, nevertheless, cunning in the stars, it was not unknown
that the heavens wore an aspect of ill; and to me, the Greek
Oinos, among others, it was evident that now had arrived the
alternation of that seven hundred and ninety-fourth year when,
at the entrance of Aries, the planet Jupiter is conjoined with the
red ring of the terrible Saturnus. The peculiar spirit of the skies,
if I mistake not greatly, made itself manifest, not only in the
physical orb of the earth, but in the souls, imaginations, and

meditations of mankind.

Over some flasks of the red Chian wine, within the walls of a noble hall, in a dim city called Ptolemais, we sat, at night, a company of seven. And to our chamber there was no entrance save by a lofty door of brass: and the door was fashioned by the artisan Corinnos,* and, being of rare workmanship, was fastened from within. Black draperies, likewise, in the gloomy room, shut out from our view the moon, the lurid stars, and the peopleless streets — but the boding and the memory of Evil, they would not be so excluded. There were things around us and about of which I can render no distinct account — things material and spiritual — heaviness in the atmosphere — a sense of suffocation — anxiety — and, above all, that terrible state of existence which the nervous experience when the senses are keenly living and awake, and meanwhile the powers of thought lie dormant. A dead-weight hung upon us. It hung upon our limbs — upon the household furniture — upon the goblets from which we drank; and all things were depressed, and borne down thereby — all things save only the flames of the seven iron lamps which illumined our revel. Uprearing themselves in tall slender lines of light, they thus remained burning all pallid and motionless; and in the mirror which their lustre formed upon the round table of ebony at which we sat, each of us there assembled beheld the pallor of his own countenance, and the unquiet glare in the downcast eyes of his companions. Yet we laughed and were merry in our proper way — which was hysterical; and sang the songs of Anacreon — which are madness; and drank deeply — although the purple wine reminded us of blood. For there was yet another tenant of our chamber in the person of young Zoilus. Dead, and at full length he lay, enshrouded; — the genius and the demon of the scene. Alas! he bore no portion in our mirth, save that his countenance, distorted with the plague, and his eyes in which Death had but half extinguished the fire of the pestilence, seemed to take such interest in our merriment as the dead may haply take in the merriment of those who are to die. But although I, Oinos, felt that the eyes of the departed were upon me, still I forced myself not to perceive the bitterness of their expression, and, gazing down steadily into the depths of the ebony mirror, sang with a loud and sonorous voice the songs of the son of Teios. But gradually my songs they ceased, and their echoes, rolling afar off among the sable draperies of the chamber, became weak, and undistinguishable, and so faded away. And lo! from among those sable draperies where the sounds of the song departed, there came forth a dark and undefined shadow — a shadow such as the moon, when low in heaven, might fashion from the figure of a man: but it was the shadow neither of man, nor of God, nor of any familiar thing. And, quivering awhile among the draperies of the room, it at length rested in full view upon the surface of the door of brass.

But the shadow was vague, and formless, and indefinite, and was the shadow neither of man nor God — neither God of Greece, nor God of Chaldæa, nor any Egyptian God. And the shadow rested upon the brazen doorway, and under the arch of the entablature of the door, and moved not, nor spoke any word, but there became stationary and remained. And the door whereupon the shadow rested was, if I remember aright, over against the feet of the young Zoilus enshrouded. But we, the seven there assembled, having seen the shadow as it came out from among the draperies, dared not steadily behold it, but cast down our eyes, and gazed continually into the depths of the mirror of ebony. And at length I, Oinos, speaking some low words, demanded of the shadow its dwelling and its appellation. And the shadow answered, "I am SHADOW, and my dwelling is near to the Catacombs of Ptolemais, and hard by those dim plains of Helusion which border upon the foul Charonian canal." And then did we, the seven, start from our seats in horror, and stand trembling, and shuddering, and aghast: for the tones in the voice of the shadow were not the tones of any one being, but of a multitude of beings, and, varying in their cadences from syllable to syllable, fell duskily upon our ears in the well remembered and familiar accents of many thousand departed friends.

THE MASQUE OF THE RED DEATH

The "Red Death" had long devastated the country. No pestilence had ever been so fatal, or so hideous. Blood* was its Avatar and its seal — the redness and the horror of blood. There were sharp pains, and sudden dizziness, and then profuse bleeding at the pores, with dissolution. The scarlet stains upon the body and especially upon the face of the victim, were the pest ban which shut him out from the aid and from the sympathy of his fellowmen. And the whole seizure, progress and termination of the disease, were the incidents of half an hour.

But the Prince Prospero was happy and dauntless and sagacious. When his dominions were half depopulated, he summoned to his presence a thousand hale and light-hearted friends from among the knights and dames of his court, and with these retired to the deep seclusion of one of his castellated abbeys. This was an extensive and magnificent structure, the creation of the prince's own eccentric yet august taste. A strong and lofty wall girdled it in. This wall had gates of iron. The courtiers, having entered, brought furnaces and massy hammers and welded the bolts. They resolved to leave means neither of ingress or egress to the sudden impulses of despair or of frenzy from within. The abbey was amply provisioned. With such precautions the courtiers might bid defiance to contagion. The external world could take care of itself. In the meantime it was folly to grieve, or to think. The prince had provided all the appliances 25 of pleasure. There were buffoons, there were improvisatori, there were ballet-dancers, there were musicians,* there was Beauty, there was wine. All these and security were within. Without was the "Red Death."

It was toward the close of the fifth or sixth month of his 30 seclusion, and while the pestilence raged most furiously abroad, that the Prince Prospero entertained his thousand friends at a masked ball of the most unusual magnificence.

It was a voluptuous scene, that masquerade. But first let me tell of the rooms in which it was held. There were seven — an 35 imperial suite. In many palaces, however, such suites form a long and straight vista, while the folding doors slide back nearly to the walls on either hand, so that the view of the whole extent is scarcely impeded. Here the case was very different; as might have been expected from the duke's love of the *bizarre*. The 40 apartments were so irregularly disposed that the vision embraced but little more than one at a time. There was a sharp turn at every twenty or thirty yards, and at each turn a novel effect. To the right and left, in the middle of each wall, a tall and narrow Gothic window looked out upon a closed corridor which 45 pursued the windings of the suite. These windows were of stained glass whose color varied in accordance with the prevailing hue of the decorations of the chamber into which it opened. That at the eastern extremity was hung, for example, in blue — and vividly blue were its windows. The second chamber was purple in its ornaments and tapestries, and here the panes were purple. The third was green throughout, and so were the casements. The fourth was furnished and lighted with orange — the fifth with white — the sixth with violet. The seventh apartment was closely shrouded in black velvet tapestries that hung all over the ceiling and down the walls, falling in heavy folds upon a carpet of the same material and hue. But in this chamber only, the color of the windows failed to correspond with the decorations. The panes here were scarlet — a deep blood color. Now in no one of the seven apartments was there any lamp or candelabrum, amid the profusion of golden ornaments that lay scattered to and fro or depended from the roof. There was no light of any kind emanating from lamp or candle within the suite of chambers. But in the corridors that followed the suite, there stood, opposite to each window, a heavy tripod, bearing a brazier of fire that projected its rays through the tinted glass and so glaringly illumined the room. And thus were produced a multitude of gaudy and fantastic appearances. But in the western or black chamber the effect of the fire-light that streamed upon the dark hangings through the blood-tinted panes, was ghastly in the extreme, and produced so wild a look upon the countenances of those who entered, that there were few of the company bold enough to set foot within its precincts at all.

It was in this apartment, also, that there stood against the western wall, a gigantic clock of ebony. Its pendulum swung to and fro with a dull, heavy, monotonous clang; and when the minute-hand made the circuit of the face, and the hour was to be stricken, there came from the brazen lungs of the clock a sound which was clear and loud and deep and exceedingly musical, but of so peculiar a note and emphasis that, at each lapse of an hour, the musicians of the orchestra were constrained to pause, momentarily, in their performance, to harken to the sound; and thus the waltzers* perforce ceased their evolutions; and there was a brief disconcert of the whole gay company; and, while the chimes of the clock yet rang, it was observed that the giddiest grew pale, and the more aged and sedate passed their hands over their brows as if in confused revery or meditation. But when the echoes had fully ceased, a light laughter at once pervaded the assembly; the musicians looked at each other and smiled as if at their own nervousness and folly, and made whispering vows, each to the other, that the next chiming of the clock should produce in them no similar emotion; and then, after the lapse of sixty minutes, (which embrace three thousand and six hundred seconds of the Time that flies,) there came yet another chiming of the clock, and then were the same disconcert and tremulousness and meditation as before.

But, in spite of these things, it was a gay and magnificent revel. The tastes of the duke were peculiar. He had a fine eye for colors and effects. He disregarded the *decora* of mere fashion. His plans were bold and fiery, and his conceptions glowed with barbaric lustre. There are some who would have thought him mad. His followers felt that he was not. It was necessary to hear and see and touch him to be *sure* that he was not.

He had directed, in great part, the moveable embellishments of the seven chambers, upon occasion of this great *fête*; and it was his own guiding taste which had given character to the masqueraders. Be sure they were grotesque. There were much glare and glitter and piquancy and phantasm — much of what has been since seen in "Hernani."* There were arabesque figures with unsuited limbs and appointments. There were delirious fancies such as the madman fashions. There were much of the beautiful, much of the wanton, much of the *bizarre*, something of the terrible, and not a little of that which might have excited disgust. To and fro in the seven chambers there stalked, in fact, a multitude of dreams. And these — the dreams — writhed in and about, taking hue from the rooms, and causing the wild music of the orchestra to seem as the echo of their steps. And, anon, there strikes the ebony clock which stands in the hall of the velvet. And then, for a moment, all is still, and all is silent save the voice of the clock. The dreams are stiff-frozen as they stand. But the echoes of the chime die away — they have endured but an instant — and a light, half-subdued laughter floats after them as they depart. And now again the music swells, and the dreams live, and writhe to and fro more merrily than ever, taking hue from the many tinted windows through which stream the rays from the tripods. But to the chamber which lies most westwardly of the seven, there are now none of the maskers who venture; for the night is waning away; and there flows a ruddier light through the blood-colored panes; and the blackness of the sable drapery appals; and to him whose foot falls upon the sable carpet, there comes from the near clock of ebony a muffled peal more solemnly emphatic than any which reaches *their* ears who indulge in the more remote gaieties of the other apartments.

But these other apartments were densely crowded, and in them beat feverishly the heart of life. And the revel went whirlingly on, until at length there commenced the sounding of midnight upon the clock. And then the music ceased, as I have told; and the evolutions of the waltzers were quieted; and there was an uneasy cessation of all things as before. But now there were twelve strokes to be sounded by the bell of the clock; and thus it happened, perhaps, that more of thought crept, with more of time, into the meditations of the thoughtful among those who revelled. And thus, too, it happened, perhaps, that before the last echoes of the last chime had utterly sunk into silence, there were many individuals in the crowd who had found leisure to become aware of the presence of a masked figure which had arrested the attention of no single individual before. And the rumor of this new presence having spread itself whisperingly around, there arose at length from the whole company a buzz, or murmur, expressive of disapprobation and surprise — then, finally, of terror, of horror, and of disgust.

In an assembly of phantasms such as I have painted, it may well be supposed that no ordinary appearance could have excited such sensation. In truth the masquerade license of the night was nearly unlimited; but the figure in question had out-Heroded Herod,* and gone beyond the bounds of even the prince's indefinite decorum. There are chords in the hearts of the most reckless which cannot be touched without emotion. Even with the utterly lost, to whom life and death are equally jests, there are matters of which no jest can be made. The whole company, indeed, seemed now deeply to feel that in the costume and bearing of the stranger neither wit nor propriety existed. The figure was tall and gaunt, and shrouded from head to foot in the habiliments of the grave. The mask which concealed the visage was made so nearly to resemble the countenance of a stiffened corpse that the closest scrutiny must have had difficulty in detecting the cheat. And yet all this might have been endured, if not approved, by the mad revellers around. But the mummer had gone so far as to assume the type of the Red Death. His vesture was dabbled in *blood* — and his broad brow, with all the features of the face, was besprinkled with the scarlet horror.

When the eyes of Prince Prospero fell upon this spectral image (which with a slow and solemn movement, as if more fully to sustain its *role*, stalked to and fro among the waltzers) he was seen to be convulsed, in the first moment with a strong shudder either of terror or distaste; but, in the next, his brow reddened with rage.

" Who dares?" he demanded hoarsely of the courtiers who stood near him — "who dares insult us with this blasphemous mockery? Seize him and unmask him — that we may know whom we have to hang at sunrise, from the battlements!"

It was in the eastern or blue chamber in which stood the Prince Prospero as he uttered these words. They rang throughout the seven rooms loudly and clearly — for the prince was a bold and robust man, and the music had became hushed at the waving of his hand.

It was in the blue room where stood the prince, with a group of pale courtiers by his side. At first, as he spoke, there was a slight rushing movement of this group in the direction of the intruder, who at the moment was also near at hand, and now, with deliberate and stately step, made closer approach to the speaker. But from a certain nameless awe with which the mad assumptions of the mummer had inspired the whole party, there were found none who put forth hand to seize him; so that, unimpeded, he passed within a yard of the prince's person; and, while the vast assembly, as if with one impulse, shrank from the centres of the rooms to the walls, he made his way uninterruptedly, but with the same solemn and measured step which had distinguished him from the first, through the blue chamber to the purple — through the purple to the green — through the green to the orange — through this again to the white — and even thence to the violet, ere a decided movement had been made to arrest him. It was then, however, that the Prince Prospero, maddening with rage and the shame of his own momentary cowardice, rushed hurriedly through the six chambers, while none followed him on account of a deadly terror that had seized upon all. He bore aloft a drawn dagger, and had approached, in rapid impetuosity, to within three or four feet of the retreating figure, when the latter, having attained the extremity of the velvet apartment, turned suddenly and confronted his pursuer. There was a sharp cry — and the dagger dropped gleaming upon the sable carpet, upon which, instantly afterwards, fell prostrate in death the Prince Prospero. Then, summoning the wild courage of despair, a throng of the revellers at once threw themselves into the black apartment, and, seizing the mummer, whose tall figure stood erect and motionless within the shadow of the ebony clock, gasped in unutterable horror at finding the grave cerements and corpselike mask which they handled with so violent a rudeness, untenanted by any tangible form.

And now was acknowledged the presence of the Red Death. He had come like a thief in the night.* And one by one dropped the revellers in the blood-bedewed halls of their revel, and died 225 each in the despairing posture of his fall. And the life of the ebony clock went out with that of the last of the gay. And the flames of the tripods expired. And Darkness and Decay and the Red Death held illimitable dominion over all.

THE DEVIL IN THE BELFRY*

What o'clock is it? — *Old Saying.*

Everybody knows, in a general way, that the finest place in the world is — or, alas, *was* — the Dutch borough* of Vondervotteimittiss.
5 Yet, as it lies some distance from any of the main roads, being in a somewhat out-of-the-way situation, there are, perhaps, very few of my readers who have ever paid it a visit. For the benefit of those who have *not*, therefore, it will be only proper that I should enter into some account of it. And this is, indeed, the more
10 necessary, as with the hope of enlisting public sympathy in behalf of the inhabitants, I design here to give a history of the calamitous events which have so lately occurred within its limits. No one who knows me will doubt that the duty thus self-imposed will be executed to the best of my ability, with all that
15 rigid impartiality, all that cautious examination into facts, and diligent collation of authorities, which should ever distinguish him who aspires to the title of historian.

By the united aid of medals, manuscripts, and inscriptions, I am enabled to say, positively, that the borough of Vondervotteimittiss
20 has existed, from its origin, in precisely the same condition which it at present preserves. Of the date of this origin, however, I grieve that I can only speak with that species of indefinite

definiteness which mathematicians are, at times, forced to put up with in certain algebraic formulæ. The date, I may thus say, in regard to the remoteness of its antiquity, cannot be less than any assignable quantity whatsoever.

Touching the derivation of the name Vondervotteimittiss, I confess myself, with sorrow, equally at fault. Among a multitude of opinions upon this delicate point — some acute, some learned, some sufficiently the reverse — I am able to select nothing which ought to be considered satisfactory. Perhaps the idea of Grogswigg — nearly coincident with that of Kroutaplenttey — is to be cautiously preferred: — It runs: — "*Vondervotteimittiss* — *Vonder, lege Donder* — *Votteimittiss, quasi und Bleitziz* — *Bleitziz obsol: pro Blitzen.*" This derivation, to say the truth, is still countenanced by some traces of the electric fluid evident on the summit of the steeple of the House of the Town-Council. I do not choose, however, to commit myself on a theme of such importance, and must refer the reader desirous of information, to the "*Oratiuncitlæ de Rebus Præter-Veteris,*" of Dundergutz. See, also, Blunderbuzzard "*De Derivationibus,*" pp. 27 to 5010, Folio, Gothic edit., Red and Black character, Catch-word and No Cypher; — wherein consult, also, marginal notes in the autograph of Stuffundpuff, with the Sub-Commentaries of Gruntundguzzell.

Notwithstanding the obscurity which thus envelops the date of the foundation of Vondervotteimittiss, and the derivation of its name, there can be no doubt, as I said before, that it has always existed as we find it at this epoch. The oldest man in the borough can remember not the slightest difference in the appearance of any portion of it; and, indeed, the very suggestion of such a possibility is considered an insult. The site of the village is in a perfectly circular valley, about a quarter of a mile in circumference, and entirely surrounded by gentle hills, over whose summit the people have never yet ventured to pass. For this they assign the very good reason that they do not believe there is anything at all on the other side.

Round the skirts of the valley, (which is quite level, and paved throughout with flat tiles,) extends a continuous row of sixty little houses. These, having their backs on the hills, must look, of course, to the centre of the plain, which is just sixty yards from the front door of each dwelling. Every house has a small garden before it, with a circular path, a sun-dial, and twenty-four cabbages. The buildings themselves are so precisely alike, that one can in no manner be distinguished from the other. Owing to the vast antiquity, the style of architecture is somewhat odd, but it is not for that reason the less strikingly picturesque. They are fashioned of hard-burned little bricks, red, with black ends, so that the walls look like a chess-board upon a great scale. The gables are turned to the front, and there are cornices, as big as all the rest of the house, over the eaves and over the main doors. The windows are narrow and deep, with very tiny panes and a great deal of sash. On the roof is a vast quantity of tiles with long curly ears. The woodwork, throughout, is of a dark hue, and there is much carving about it, with but a trifling variety of pattern; for, time out of mind, the carvers of Vondervotteimittiss have never been able to carve more than two objects — a time-piece and a cabbage. But these they do exceedingly well, and intersperse them, with singular ingenuity, wherever they find room for the chisel.

The dwellings are as much alike inside as out, and the furniture is all upon one plan. The floors are of square tiles, the chairs and tables of black-looking wood with thin crooked legs and puppy feet. The mantel-pieces are wide and high, and have not only time-pieces and cabbages sculptured over the front, but a real time-piece, which makes a prodigious ticking, on the top in the middle, with a flower-pot containing a cabbage standing on each extremity by way of outrider. Between each cabbage and the time-piece, again, is a little China man having a large stomach with a great round hole in it, through which is seen the dial-plate of a watch.

The fire-places are large and deep, with fierce crooked-looking fire-dogs. There is constantly a rousing fire, and a huge pot over it, full of sauer-kraut and pork, to which the good woman of the house is always busy in attending. She is a little fat old lady, with blue eyes and a red face, and wears a huge cap like a sugar-loaf, ornamented with purple and yellow ribbons. Her dress is of orange-colored linsey-woolsey, made very full behind and very short in the waist — and indeed very short in other respects, not reaching below the middle of her leg. This is somewhat thick, and so are her ankles, but she has a fine pair of green stockings to cover them. Her shoes — of pink leather — are fastened each with a bunch of yellow ribbons puckered up in the shape of a cabbage. In her left hand she has a little heavy Dutch watch; in her right she wields a ladle for the sauer-kraut and pork. By her side there stands a fat tabby cat, with a gilt toy repeater tied to its tail, which "the boys" have there fastened by way of a quiz.

The boys themselves are, all three of them, in the garden attending the pig. They are each two feet in height. They have three-cornered cocked hats, purple waistcoats reaching down to their thighs, buckskin knee-breeches, red woollen stockings, heavy shoes with big silver buckles, and long surtout coats with large buttons of mother-of-pearl. Each, too, has a pipe in his mouth, and a little dumpy watch in his right hand. He takes a puff and a look, and then a look and a puff. The pig — which is corpulent and lazy — is occupied now in picking up the stray leaves that fall from the cabbages, and now in giving a kick behind at the gilt repeater, which the urchins have also tied to *his* tail, in order to make him look as handsome as the cat.

Right at the front door, in a high-backed leather-bottomed armed chair, with crooked legs and puppy feet like the tables, is seated the old man of the house himself. He is an exceedingly puffy little old gentleman, with big circular eyes and a huge double chin. His dress resembles that of the boys — and I need say nothing farther about it. All the difference is, that his pipe is somewhat bigger than theirs, and he can make a greater smoke. Like them, he has a watch, but he carries his watch in his pocket. To say the truth, he has something of more importance than a watch to attend to — and what that is, I shall presently explain. He sits with his right leg upon his left knee, wears a grave countenance, and always keeps one of his eyes, at least, resolutely bent upon a certain remarkable object in the centre of the plain.

This object is situated in the steeple of the House of the Town-Council. The Town-Council are all very little, round, oily, intelligent men, with big saucer eyes and fat double chins, and have their coats much longer and their shoe-buckles much bigger than the ordinary inhabitants of Vondervotteimittiss. Since my sojourn in the borough, they have had several special meetings, and have adopted these three important resolutions: —

"That it is wrong to alter the good old course of things:"

"That there is nothing tolerable out of Vondervotteimittiss:" and —

"That we will stick by our clocks and our cabbages."

Above the session-room of the Council is the steeple, and in the steeple is the belfry, where exists, and has existed time out of mind, the pride and wonder of the village — the great clock of the

borough of Vondervotteimittiss. And this is the object to which the eyes of the old gentlemen are turned who sit in the leather-
150   bottomed arm chairs.

The great clock has seven faces — one in each of the seven sides of the steeple — so that it can be readily seen from all quarters. Its faces are large and white, and its hands heavy and black. There is a belfry-man whose sole duty is to attend to it;
155   but this duty is the most perfect of sinecures — for the clock of Vondervotteimittiss was never yet known to have anything the matter with it. Until lately, the bare supposition of such a thing was considered heretical. From the remotest period of antiquity to which the archives have reference, the hours have been
160   regularly struck by the big bell. And, indeed, the case was just the same with all the other clocks and watches in the borough. Never was such a place for keeping the true time. When the large clapper thought proper to say "Twelve o'clock!" all its obedient followers opened their throats simultaneously, and
165   responded like a very echo. In short, the good burghers were fond of their sauer-kraut, but then they were proud of their clocks.

All people who hold sinecure offices are held in more or less respect, and as the belfry-man of Vondervotteimittiss has the
170   most perfect of sinecures, he is the most perfectly respected of any man in the world. He is the chief dignitary of the borough, and the very pigs look up to him with a sentiment of reverence.

His coat-tail is *very* far longer — his pipe, his shoe-buckles, his eyes, and his stomach, *very* far bigger — than those of any other old gentleman in the village; and as to his chin, it is not only double, but triple.

I have thus painted the happy estate of Vondervotteimittiss: alas, that so fair a picture should ever experience a reverse!

There has been long a saying among the wisest inhabitants, that "no good can come from over the hills;" and it really seemed that the words had in them something of the spirit of prophecy. It wanted five minutes of noon, on the day before yesterday, when there appeared a very odd-looking object on the summit of the ridge to the eastward. Such an occurrence, of course, attracted universal attention, and every little old gentleman who sat in a leather-bottomed arm-chair, turned one of his eyes with a stare of dismay upon the phenomenon, still keeping the other upon the clock in the steeple.

By the time that it wanted only three minutes to noon, the droll object in question was perceived to be a very diminutive foreign-looking young man. He descended the hills at a great rate, so that everybody had soon a good look at him. He was really the most finnicky little personage that had ever been seen in Vondervotteimittiss. His countenance was of a dark snuff-color, and he had a long hooked nose, pea eyes, a wide mouth, and an excellent set of teeth, which latter he seemed anxious of displaying, as he was grinning from ear to ear. What with mustachios and whiskers, there was none of the rest of his face to be seen. His head was uncovered, and his hair neatly done up in *papillotes*. His dress was a tight-fitting swallow-tailed black coat, (from one of whose pockets dangled a vast length of white handkerchief,) black kerseymere knee-breeches, black stockings, and stumpy-looking pumps, with huge bunches of black satin ribbon for bows. Under one arm he carried a huge *chapeau-de-bras*, and under the other a fiddle nearly five times as big as himself. In his left hand was a gold snuff-box, from which, as he capered down the hill, cutting all manner of fantastical steps, he took snuff incessantly with an air of the greatest possible self-satisfaction. God bless me! — here was a sight for the honest burghers of Vondervotteimittiss!

To speak plainly, the fellow had, in spite of his grinning, an audacious and sinister kind of face; and as he curvetted right into the village, the odd stumpy appearance of his pumps excited no little suspicion; and many a burgher who beheld him that day, would have given a trifle for a peep beneath the white cambric handkerchief which hung so obtrusively from the pocket of his swallow-tailed coat. But what mainly occasioned a righteous indignation was, that the scoundrelly popinjay, while he cut a fandango here, and a whirligig there, did not seem to have the remotest idea in the world of such a thing as *keeping time* in his steps.

The good people of the borough had scarcely a chance, however, to get their eyes thoroughly open, when, just as it wanted half a minute of noon, the rascal bounced, as I say, right into the midst of them; gave a *chassez*, here, and a *balancez* there; and then, after a *pirouette* and a *pas-de-zéphyr*, pigeon-winged himself right up into the belfry of the House of the Town-Council, where the wonder-stricken belfry-man sat smoking in a state of dignity and dismay. But the little chap seized him at once by the nose; gave it a swing and a pull; clapped the big *chapeau-de-bras* upon his head; knocked it down over his eyes and mouth; and then, lifting up the big fiddle, beat him with it so long and so soundly, that what with the belfry-man being so fat, and the fiddle being so hollow, you would have sworn that there was a regiment of double-bass drummers all beating the devil's tattoo* up in the belfry of the steeple of Vondervotteimittiss.

There is no knowing to what desperate act of vengeance this unprincipled attack might have aroused the inhabitants, but for the important fact that it now wanted only half a second of noon. The bell was about to strike, and it was a matter of absolute and pre-eminent necessity that every body should look well at his watch. It was evident, however, that just at this moment, the fellow in the steeple was doing something that he had no business to do with the clock. But as it now began to strike, nobody had any time to attend to his manœuvres, for they had all to count the strokes of the bell as it sounded.

"One!" said the clock.

"Von!" echoed every little old gentleman in every leather-bottomed arm-chair in Vondervotteimittiss. "Von!" said his watch also; "von!" said the watch of his vrow, and "von!" said the watches of the boys, and the little gilt repeaters on the tails of the cat and pig.

"Two!" continued the big bell; and

"Doo!" repeated all the repeaters.

"Three! Four! Five! Six! Seven! Eight! Nine! Ten!" said the bell.

"Dree! Vour! Fibe! Sax! Seben! Aight! Noin! Den!" answered the others.

"Eleven!" said the big one.

"Eleben!" assented the little fellows.

"Twelve!" said the bell.

"Dvelf!" they replied, perfectly satisfied, and dropping their voices.

"Und dvelf it iss!" said all the little old gentlemen, putting up their watches. But the big bell had not done with them yet.

"*Thirteen!* " said he.

" Der Teufel!" gasped the little old gentlemen, turning pale, dropping their pipes, and putting down all their right legs from over their left knees.

"Der Teufel!" groaned they, "Dirteen! Dirteen!! — Mein Gott, it is Dirteen o'clock!!"*

Why attempt to describe the terrible scene which ensued? All Vondervotteimittiss flew at once into a lamentable state of uproar.

"Vot is cum'd to mein pelly?" roared all the boys, — "I've been ongry for dis hour!"

"Vot is cum'd to mein kraut?" screamed all the vrows, "It has been done to rags for dis hour!"

"Vot is cum'd to mein pipe?" swore all the little old gentlemen, "Donder and Blitzen! it has been smoked out for dis hour!" — and they filled them up again in a great rage, and, sinking back in their arm-chairs, puffed away so fast and so fiercely that the whole valley was immediately filled with impenetrable smoke.

Meantime the cabbages all turned very red in the face, and it seemed as if old Nick* himself had taken possession of everything in the shape of a time-piece. The clocks carved upon the furniture took to dancing as if bewitched, while those upon the mantelpieces could scarcely contain themselves for fury, and kept such a continual striking of thirteen, and such a frisking and wriggling of their pendulums as was really horrible to see. But, worse than all, neither the cats nor the pigs could put up any longer with the behavior of the little repeaters tied to their tails, and resented it by scampering all over the place, scratching and poking, and squeaking and screeching, and caterwauling and squalling, and flying into the faces, and running under the petticoats of the people, and creating altogether the most abominable din and confusion which it is possible for a reasonable person to conceive. And to make matters still more distressing, the rascally little scapegrace in the steeple was evidently exerting himself to the utmost. Every now and then one might catch a glimpse of the scoundrel through the smoke. There he sat in the belfry upon the belfry-man, who was lying flat upon his back. In his teeth the villain held the bell-rope, which he kept jerking about with his head, raising such a clatter that my ears ring again even to think of it. On his lap lay the big fiddle at which he was scraping out of all time and tune, with both hands, making a great show, the nincompoop! of playing "Judy O'Flannagan" and "Paddy O'Raferty."

Affairs being thus miserably situated, I left the place in disgust, and now appeal for aid to all lovers of correct time and fine kraut. Let us proceed in a body to the borough, and restore the ancient order of things in Vondervotteimittiss by ejecting that little fellow from the steeple.

A TALE OF THE RAGGED MOUNTAINS

During the fall of the year 1827, while residing near Charlottesville, Virginia, I casually made the acquaintance of Mr. Augustus Bedloe. This young gentleman was remarkable in every respect, and excited in me a profound interest and curiosity. I found it impossible to comprehend him either in his moral or his physical relations. Of his family I could obtain no satisfactory account. Whence he came, I never ascertained. Even about his age — although I call him a young gentleman — there was something which perplexed me in no little degree. He certainly *seemed* young — and he made a point of speaking about his youth — yet there were moments when I should have had little trouble in imagining him a hundred years of age. But in no regard was he more peculiar than in his personal appearance. He was singularly tall and thin. He stooped much. His limbs were exceedingly long and emaciated. His forehead was broad and low. His complexion was absolutely bloodless. His mouth was large and flexible, and his teeth were more wildly uneven, although sound, than I had ever before seen teeth in a human head. The expression of his smile, however, was by no means unpleasing, as might be supposed; but it had no variation whatever. It was one of profound melancholy — of a phaseless and unceasing gloom. His eyes were abnormally large, and round like those of a cat. The pupils, too, upon any accession or diminution of light, underwent contraction or dilation, just such as is observed in the feline tribe. In moments of excitement the orbs grew bright to a degree almost inconceivable; seeming to emit luminous rays, not of a reflected, but of an intrinsic lustre, as does a candle or the sun; yet their ordinary condition was so totally vapid, filmy and dull, as to convey the idea of the eyes of a long-interred corpse.

These peculiarities of person appeared to cause him much annoyance, and he was continually alluding to them in a sort of half explanatory, half apologetic strain, which, when I first heard it, impressed me very painfully. I soon, however, grew accustomed to it, and my uneasiness wore off. It seemed to be his design rather to insinuate than directly to assert that, physically, he had not always been what he was — that a long series of neuralgic attacks had reduced him from a condition of more than usual personal beauty, to that which I saw. For many years past he bad been attended by a physician, named Templeton — an old gentleman, perhaps seventy years of age — whom he had first encountered at Saratoga,* and from whose attention, while there, he either received, or fancied that he received, great benefit. The result was that Bedloe, who was wealthy, had made an arrangement with Doctor Templeton, by which the latter, in consideration of a liberal annual allowance, had consented to devote his time and medical experience exclusively to the care of the invalid.

Doctor Templeton had been a traveller in his younger days, and, at Paris, had become a convert, in great measure, to the doctrines of Mesmer.* It was altogether by means of magnetic remedies that he had succeeded in alleviating the acute pains of his patient; and this success had very naturally inspired the latter with a certain degree of confidence in the opinions from which the remedies had been educed. The Doctor, however, like all enthusiasts, had struggled hard to make a thorough convert of his pupil, and finally so far gained his point as to induce the sufferer to submit to numerous experiments. By a frequent repetition of these, a result had arisen, which of late days has become so common as to attract little or no attention, but which, at the period of which I write, had very rarely been known in America. I mean to say, that between Doctor Templeton and Bedloe there had grown up, little by little, a very distinct and strongly marked *rapport*, or magnetic relation. I am not prepared to assert, however, that this *rapport* extended beyond the limits of the simple sleep-producing power; but this power itself had attained great intensity. At the first attempt to induce the magnetic somnolency, the mesmerist entirely failed. In the fifth or sixth he succeeded very partially, and after long continued effort. Only at the twelfth was the triumph complete. After this the will of the patient succombed rapidly to that of the physician, so that, when I first became acquainted with the two, sleep was brought about almost instantaneously, by the mere volition of the operator, even when the invalid was unaware of his presence. It is only now, in the year 1845, when similar miracles are witnessed 75 daily by thousands, that I dare venture to record this apparent impossibility as a matter of serious fact.*

The temperament of Bedloe was, in the highest degree, sensitive, excitable, enthusiastic. His imagination was singularly vigorous and creative; and no doubt it derived additional force 80 from the habitual use of morphine, which he swallowed in great quantity, and without which he would have found it impossible to exist. It was his practice to take a very large dose of it immediately after breakfast, each morning — or rather immediately after a cup of strong coffee, for he ate nothing in the forenoon — 85 and then set forth alone, or attended only by a dog, upon a long ramble among the chain of wild and dreary hills that lie westward and southward of Charlottesville, and are there dignified by the title of the Ragged Mountains.

Upon a dim, warm, misty day, towards the close of November, 90 and during the strange *interregnum* of the seasons which in America is termed the Indian Summer, Mr. Bedloe departed, as usual, for the hills. The day passed, and still he did not return.

About eight o'clock at night, having become seriously alarmed at his protracted absence, we were about setting out in search of 95 him, when he unexpectedly made his appearance, in health no worse than usual, and in rather more than ordinary spirits. The account which he gave of his expedition, and of the events which had detained him, was a singular one indeed.

100   "You will remember," said he, "that it was about nine in the morning when I left Charlottesville. I bent my steps immediately to the mountains, and, about ten, entered a gorge which was entirely new to me. I followed the windings of this pass with much interest. The scenery which presented itself on all sides,
105   although scarcely entitled to be called grand, had about it an indescribable, and to me, a delicious aspect of dreary desolation. The solitude seemed absolutely virgin. I could not help believing that the green sods and the gray rocks upon which I trod, had been trodden never before by the foot of a human being. So
110   entirely secluded, and in fact inaccessible, except through a series of accidents, is the entrance of the ravine, that it is by no means impossible that I was indeed the first adventurer — the very first and sole adventurer who had ever penetrated its recesses.

115   "The thick and peculiar mist, or smoke, which distinguishes the Indian Summer, and which now hung heavily over all objects, served, no doubt, to deepen the vague impressions which these objects created. So dense was this pleasant fog, that I could at no time see more than a dozen yards of the path
120   before me. This path was excessively sinuous, and as the sun could not be seen, I soon lost all idea of the direction in which I journeyed. In the meantime the morphine had its customary

effect — that of enduing all the external world with an intensity of interest. In the quivering of a leaf — in the hue of a blade of grass — in the shape of a trefoil — in the humming of a bee — in 125 the gleaming of a dew-drop — in the breathing of the wind — in the faint odors that came from the forest — there came a whole universe of suggestion — a gay and motley train of rhapsodical and immethodical thought.

"Busied in this, I walked on for several hours, during which the 130 mist deepened around me to so great an extent, that at length I was reduced to an absolute groping of the way. And now an indescribable uneasiness possessed me — a species of nervous hesitation and tremor. I feared to tread, lest I should be precipitated into some abyss. I remembered, too, strange stories 135 told about these Ragged Hills, and of the uncouth and fierce races of men who tenanted their groves and caverns. A thousand vague fancies oppressed and disconcerted me — fancies the more distressing because vague. Very suddenly my attention was arrested by the loud beating of a drum. 140

"My amazement was, of course, extreme. A drum in these hills was a thing unknown. I could not have been more surprised at the sound of the trump of the Archangel.* But a new and still more astounding source of interest and perplexity arose. There came a wild rattling or jingling sound, as if of a bunch of large 145 keys — and upon the instant a dusky-visaged and half-naked man rushed past me with a shriek. He came so close to my person that I felt his hot breath upon my face. He bore in one hand an instrument composed of an assemblage of steel rings, 150 and shook them vigorously as he ran. Scarcely had he disappeared in the mist, before, panting after him, with open mouth and glaring eyes, there darted a huge beast. I could not be mistaken in its character. It was a hyena.

"The sight of this monster rather relieved than heightened my 155 terrors — for I now made sure that I dreamed, and endeavored to arouse myself to waking consciousness. I stepped boldly and briskly forward. I rubbed my eyes. I called aloud. I pinched my limbs. A small spring of water presented itself to my view, and here, stooping, I bathed my hands and my head and neck. This 160 seemed to dissipate the equivocal sensations which had hitherto annoyed me. I arose, as I thought, a new man, and proceeded steadily and complacently on my unknown way.

"At length, quite overcome by exertion, and by a certain oppressive closeness of the atmosphere, I seated myself beneath a tree. 165 Presently there came a feeble gleam of sunshine and the shadow of the leaves of the tree fell faintly but definitely upon the grass. At this shadow I gazed wonderingly for many minutes. Its character stupified me with astonishment. I looked upward. The tree was a palm.

170 "I now arose hurriedly, and in a state of fearful agitation — for the fancy that I dreamed would serve me no longer. I saw — I felt that I had perfect command of my senses — and these

senses now brought to my soul a world of novel and singular sensation. The heat became all at once intolerable. A strange odor loaded the breeze. A low continuous murmur, like that arising from a full, but gently-flowing river, came to my ears, intermingled with the peculiar hum of multitudinous human voices.

"While I listened in an extremity of astonishment which I need not attempt to describe, a strong and brief gust of wind bore off the incumbent fog as if by the wand of an enchanter.

"I found myself at the foot of a high mountain, and looking down into a vast plain, through which wound a majestic river. On the margin of this river stood an Eastern-looking city, such as we read of in the Arabian Tales, but of a character even more singular than any there described. From my position, which was far above the level of the town, I could perceive its every nook and corner, as if delineated on a map. The streets seemed innumerable, and crossed each other irregularly in all directions, but were rather long winding alleys than streets, and absolutely swarmed with inhabitants. The houses were wildly picturesque. On every hand was a wilderness of balconies, of verandahs, of minarets, of shrines, and fantastically carved oriels. Bazaars abounded; and in these were displayed rich wares in infinite variety and profusion — silks, muslins, the most dazzling cutlery, the most magnificent jewels and gems. Besides these things, were seen, on all sides, banners and palanquins, litters with stately dames close veiled, elephants gorgeously caparisoned, idols grotesquely hewn, drums, banners

200 and gongs, spears, silver and gilded maces. And amid the crowd, and the clamor, and the general intricacy and confusion — amid the million of black and yellow men, turbaned and robed, and of flowing beard, there roamed a countless multitude of holy filleted bulls, while vast legions of the filthy but sacred ape clambered,

205 chattering and shrieking, about the cornices of the mosques,* or clung to the minarets and oriels. From the swarming streets to the banks of the river, there descended innumerable flights of steps leading to bathing places, while the river itself seemed to force a passage with difficulty through the vast fleets of deeply-

210 burthened ships that far and wide encumbered its surface. Beyond the limits of the city arose, in frequent majestic groups, the palm and the cocoa, with other gigantic and weird trees of vast age; and here and there might be seen a field of rice, the thatched hut of a peasant, a tank, a stray temple, a gypsy camp,

215 or a solitary graceful maiden taking her way, with a pitcher upon her head, to the banks of the magnificent river.

"You will say now, of course, that I dreamed; but not so. What I saw — what I heard — what I felt — what I thought — had about it nothing of the unmistakeable idiosyncrasy of the dream.

220 All was rigorously self-consistent. At first, doubting that I was really awake, I entered into a series of tests, which soon convinced me that I really was. Now, when one dreams, and, in

the dream, suspects that he dreams, the suspicion *never fails to confirm itself,* and the sleeper is almost immediately aroused. Thus Novalis errs not in saying that 'we are near waking when we dream that we dream.' Had the vision occurred to me as I describe it, without my suspecting it as a dream, then a dream it might absolutely have been, but, occurring as it did, and suspected and tested as it was, I am forced to class it among other phenomena."

" In this I am not sure that you are wrong," observed Dr. Templeton, "but proceed. You arose and descended into the city."

"I arose," continued Bedloe, regarding the Doctor with an air of profound astonishment, "I arose, as you say, and descended into the city. On my way, I fell in with an immense populace, crowding, through every avenue, all in the same direction, and exhibiting in every action the wildest excitement. Very suddenly, and by some inconceivable impulse, I became intensely imbued with personal interest in what was going on. I seemed to feel that I had an important part to play, without exactly understanding what it was. Against the crowd which environed me, however, I experienced a deep sentiment of animosity. I shrank from amid them, and, swiftly, by a circuitous path, reached and entered the city. Here all was the wildest tumult and contention. A small party of men, clad in garments half Indian, half European, and officered by gentlemen in a uniform partly British, were engaged, at great odds, with the swarming rabble of the alleys. I joined the weaker party, arming myself with the weapons of a fallen officer, and fighting I knew not whom with the nervous ferocity of despair. We were soon overpowered by numbers, and driven to seek refuge in a species of kiosk. Here we barricaded ourselves, and, for the present, were secure. From a loop-hole near the summit of the kiosk, I perceived a vast, crowd, in furious agitation, surrounding and assaulting a gay palace that overhung the river. Presently, from an upper window of this palace, there descended an effeminate-looking person, by means of a string made of the turbans of his attendants. A boat was at hand, in which he escaped to the opposite bank of the river.

"And now a new object took possession of my soul. I spoke a few hurried but energetic words to my companions, and, having succeeded in gaining over a few of them to my purpose, made a frantic sally from the kiosk. We rushed amid the crowd that surrounded it. They retreated, at first, before us. They rallied, fought madly, and retreated again. In the meantime we were borne far from the kiosk, and became bewildered and entangled among the narrow streets of tall overhanging houses, into the recesses of which the sun had never been able to shine. The rabble pressed impetuously upon us, harassing us with their spears, and overwhelming us with flights of arrows. These latter were very remarkable, and resembled in some respects the writhing creese of the Malay. They were made to imitate the body of a creeping serpent, and were long and black, with a poisoned barb. One of them struck me upon the right temple. I reeled and fell. An instantaneous and deadly sickness seized me. I struggled — I gasped — I died." 275

"You will hardly persist *now*," said I, smiling, "that the whole of your adventure was not a dream. You are not prepared to maintain that you are dead?"

When I said these words, I of course expected some lively sally from Bedloe in reply; but, to my astonishment, he 280 hesitated, trembled, became fearfully pallid, and remained silent. I looked towards Templeton. He sat erect and rigid in his chair — his teeth chattered, and his eyes were starting from their sockets. "Proceed!" he at length said hoarsely to Bedloe.

"For many minutes," continued the latter, "my sole sentiment 285 — my sole feeling — was that of darkness and nonentity, with the consciousness of death. At length, there seemed to pass a violent and sudden shock through my soul, as if of electricity. With it came the sense of elasticity and of light. This latter I felt — not saw. In an instant I seemed to rise from the ground. But I 290 had no bodily, no visible, audible, or palpable presence. The crowd had departed. The tumult had ceased. The city was in comparative repose. Beneath me lay my corpse, with the arrow in my temple, the whole head greatly swollen and disfigured. But all these things I felt — not saw. I took interest in nothing. 295 Even the corpse seemed a matter in which I had no concern. Volition I had none, but appeared to be impelled into motion, and flitted buoyantly out of the city, retracing the circuitous path by which I had entered it. When I had attained that point of the ravine in the mountains, at which I had encountered the hyena, I again experienced a shock as of a galvanic battery;* the sense of weight, of volition, of substance, returned. I became my original self, and bent my steps eagerly homewards — but the past had not lost the vividness of the real — and not now, even for an instant, can I compel my understanding to regard it as a dream."

"Nor was it," said Templeton, with an air of deep solemnity, "yet it would be difficult to say how otherwise it should be termed. Let us suppose only, that the soul of the man of to-day is upon the verge of some stupendous psychal discoveries. Let us content ourselves with this supposition. For the rest I have some explanation to make. Here is a water-colour drawing, which I should have shown you before, but which an unaccountable sentiment of horror has hitherto prevented me from showing."

We looked at the picture which he presented. I saw nothing in it of an extraordinary character; but its effect upon Bedloe was prodigious. He nearly fainted as he gazed. And yet it was but a miniature portrait — a miraculously accurate one, to be sure — of his own very remarkable features. At least this was my thought as I regarded it.

"You will perceive," said Templeton, "the date of this picture — it is here, scarcely visible, in this corner — 1780. In this year was the portrait taken. It is the likeness of a dead friend — a Mr. Oldeb — to whom I became much attached at Calcutta, during the administration of Warren Hastings. I was then only twenty years old. When I first saw you, Mr. Bedloe, at Saratoga, it was the miraculous similarity which existed between yourself and the painting, which induced me to accost you, to seek your friendship, and to bring about those arrangements which resulted in my becoming your constant companion. In accomplishing this point, I was urged partly, and perhaps principally, by a regretful memory of the deceased, but also, in part, by an uneasy, and not altogether horrorless curiosity respecting yourself.

"In your detail of the vision which presented itself to you amid the hills, you have described, with the minutest accuracy, the Indian city of Benares, upon the Holy River. The riots, the combats, the massacre, were the actual events of the insurrection of Cheyte Sing, which took place in 1780, when Hastings was put in imminent peril of his life.* The man escaping by the string of turbans, was Cheyte Sing himself. The party in the kiosk were sepoys and British officers, headed by Hastings. Of this party I was one, and did all I could to prevent the rash and fatal sally of the officer who fell, in the crowded alleys, by the poisoned arrow of a Bengalee. That officer was my dearest friend. It was Oldeb. You will perceive by these manuscripts," (here the speaker produced a note-book in which several pages appeared to have been freshly written) "that at the very period in which you fancied these things amid the hills, I was engaged in detailing them upon paper here at home."

350   In about a week after this conversation, the following paragraphs appeared in a Charlottesville paper.

" We have the painful duty of announcing the death of Mr. AUGUSTUS BEDLO, a gentleman whose amiable manners and many virtues have long endeared him to the citizens of 355   Charlottesville.

"Mr. B., for some years past, has been subject to neuralgia, which has often threatened to terminate fatally; but this can be regarded only as the mediate cause of his decease. The proximate cause was one of especial singularity. In an excursion 360   to the Ragged Mountains, a few days since, a slight cold and fever were contracted, attended with great determination of blood to the head. To relieve this, Dr. Templeton resorted to topical bleeding. Leeches were applied to the temples. In a fearfully brief period the patient died, when it appeared that, in 365   the jar containing the leeches, had been introduced, by accident, one of the venomous vermicular sangsues* which are now and then found in the neighboring ponds. This creature fastened itself upon a small artery in the right temple. Its close resemblance to the medicinal leech caused the mistake to be 370   overlooked until too late.

"N. B. The poisonous sangsue of Charlottesville may always be distinguished from the medicinal leech by its blackness, and especially by its writhing or vermicular motions, which very nearly resemble those of a snake."

I was speaking with the editor of the paper in question, upon the topic of this remarkable accident, when it occurred to me to ask how it happened that the name of the deceased had been given as Bedlo.   375

"I presume," said I, "you have authority for this spelling, but I have always supposed the name to be written with an *e* at the end."   380

"Authority? — no," he replied. "It is a mere typographical error. The name is Bedloe with an *e*, all the world over, and I never knew it to be spelt otherwise in my life."

"Then," said I mutteringly, as I turned upon my heel, "then indeed has it come to pass that one truth is stranger than any fiction — for Bedlo, without the *e*, what is it but Oldeb conversed? And this man tells me it is a typographical error."   385

THE RAVEN

Once upon a midnight dreary, while I pondered, weak and weary,**
Over many a quaint and curious volume of forgotten lore —
While I nodded, nearly napping, suddenly there came a tapping,
As of some one gently rapping, rapping at my chamber door —
" 'Tis some visiter," I muttered, "tapping at my chamber door —
      Only this and nothing more."

Ah, distinctly I remember it was in the bleak December;
And each separate dying ember wrought its ghost upon the floor.
Eagerly I wished the morrow; — vainly I had sought to borrow
From my books surcease of sorrow — sorrow for the lost Lenore —
For the rare and radiant maiden whom the angels name Lenore —
      Nameless *here* for evermore.

And the silken, sad, uncertain rustling of each purple curtain
Thrilled me — filled me with fantastic terrors never felt before;
So that now, to still the beating of my heart, I stood repeating
" 'Tis some visiter entreating entrance at my chamber door —
Some late visiter entreating entrance at my chamber door; —
      This it is and nothing more."

Presently my soul grew stronger; hesitating then no longer, 20
"Sir," said I, "or Madam, truly your forgiveness I implore;
But the fact is I was napping, and so gently you came rapping,
And so faintly you came tapping, tapping at my chamber door,
That I scarce was sure I heard you" — here I opened wide the door; —
     Darkness there and nothing more. 25

Deep into that darkness peering, long I stood there wondering, fearing,
Doubting, dreaming dreams no mortal ever dared to dream before;
But the silence was unbroken, and the stillness gave no token,
And the only word there spoken was the whispered word, "Lenore?"
This I whispered, and an echo murmured back the word, "Lenore!" 30
     Merely this and nothing more.

Back into the chamber turning, all my soul within me burning,
Soon again I heard a tapping somewhat louder than before.
"Surely," said I, "surely that is something at my window lattice;
Let me see, then, what thereat is, and this mystery explore — 35
Let my heart be still a moment and this mystery explore; —
     'Tis the wind* and nothing more!"

Open here I flung the shutter, when, with many a flirt and flutter,
In there stepped a stately Raven of the saintly days of yore;
Not the least obeisance made he; not a minute stopped or stayed he; 40
But, with mien of lord or lady, perched above my chamber door —

Perched upon a bust of Pallas just above my chamber door —
> Perched, and sat, and nothing more.

Then this ebony bird beguiling my sad fancy into smiling,
45 By the grave and stern decorum of the countenance it wore,
"Though thy crest be shorn and shaven, thou," I said, "art sure no craven,
Ghastly grim and ancient Raven wandering from the Nightly shore —
Tell me what thy lordly name is on the Night's Plutonian shore!"
> Quoth the Raven "Nevermore."

50 Much I marvelled this ungainly fowl to hear discourse so plainly,
Though its answer little meaning — little relevancy bore;
For we cannot help agreeing that no living human being
Ever yet was blessed with seeing bird above his chamber door —
Bird or beast upon the sculptured bust above his chamber door,
55 > With such name as "Nevermore."

But the Raven, sitting lonely on the placid bust, spoke only
That one word, as if his soul in that one word he did outpour.
Nothing farther then he uttered — not a feather then he fluttered —
Till I scarcely more than unuttered "Other friends have flown before —
60 On the morrow *he* will leave me, as my Hopes have flown before."
> Then the bird said "Nevermore."

Startled at the stillness broken by reply so aptly spoken,

"Doubtless," said I, "what it utters is its only stock and store
Caught from some unhappy master whom unmerciful Disaster
Followed fast and followed faster till his songs one burden bore — 65
Till the dirges of his Hope that melancholy burden bore
        Of 'Never — nevermore.'"

But the Raven still beguiling my sad fancy into smiling,
Straight I wheeled a cushioned seat in front of bird, and bust and door; 70
Then, upon the velvet sinking, I betook myself to linking
Fancy unto fancy, thinking what this ominous bird of yore —
What this grim, ungainly, ghastly, gaunt, and ominous bird of yore
        Meant in croaking "Nevermore."

This I sat engaged in guessing, but no syllable expressing 75
To the fowl whose fiery eyes now burned into my bosom's core;
This and more I sat divining, with my head at ease reclining
On the cushion's velvet lining that the lamp-light gloated o'er,
But whose velvet-violet lining with the lamp-light gloating o'er,
        She shall press, ah, nevermore! 80

Then, methought, the air grew denser, perfumed from an unseen censer
Swung by seraphim whose foot-falls tinkled on the tufted floor.
"Wretch," I cried, "thy God hath lent thee — by these angels he
    hath sent thee
Respite — respite and nepenthe from thy memories of Lenore; 85

Quaff, oh quaff this kind nepenthe and forget this lost Lenore!"
>Quoth the Raven "Nevermore."

"Prophet!" said I, "thing of evil! — prophet still, if bird or devil! —
Whether Tempter sent, or whether tempest tossed thee here ashore,
90 Desolate yet all undaunted, on this desert land enchanted —
On this home by Horror haunted — tell me truly, I implore —
Is there — *is* there balm in Gilead? *— tell me — tell me, I implore!"
>Quoth the Raven "Nevermore."

"Prophet!" said I, "thing of evil! — prophet still, if bird or devil!
95 By that Heaven that bends above us — by that God we both adore —
Tell this soul with sorrow laden if, within the distant Aidenn,
It shall clasp a sainted maiden whom the angels name Lenore —
Clasp a rare and radiant maiden whom the angels name Lenore."
>Quoth the Raven "Nevermore."

100 "Be that word our sign of parting, bird or fiend!" I shrieked, upstarting —
"Get thee back into the tempest and the Night's Plutonian shore!
Leave no black plume as a token of that lie thy soul hath spoken!
Leave my loneliness unbroken! — quit the bust above my door!
Take thy beak from out my heart, and take thy form from off my door!"
105 >Quoth the Raven "Nevermore."

And the Raven, never flitting, still is sitting, *still* is sitting

On the pallid bust of Pallas just above my chamber door;

And his eyes have all the seeming of a demon's that is dreaming,

And the lamp-light o'er him streaming throws his shadow on the floor;

And my soul from out that shadow that lies floating on the floor   110

Shall be lifted — nevermore!

INSTINCT VS REASON — A BLACK CAT

The line which demarcates the instinct of the brute creation from the boasted reason of man, is, beyond doubt, of the most shadowy and unsatisfactory character — a boundary line far more difficult to settle than even the North-Eastern or the Oregon.* The question whether the lower animals do or do not reason, will possibly never be decided — certainly never in our present condition of knowledge. While the self-love and arrogance of man will persist in denying the reflective power to beasts, because the granting it seems to derogate from his own vaunted supremacy, he yet perpetually finds himself involved in the paradox of decrying instinct as an inferior faculty, while he is forced to admit its infinite superiority, in a thousand cases, over the very reason which he claims exclusively as his own. Instinct, so far from being an inferior reason, is perhaps the most exacted* intellect of all. It will appear to the true philosopher as the divine mind itself acting *immediately* upon its creatures.

The habits of the lion-ant, of many kinds of spiders, and of the beaver, have in them a wonderful analogy, or rather similarity, to the usual operations of the reason of man — but the instinct of some other creatures has no such analogy — and is referable only to the spirit of the Deity itself, acting *directly*, and through no corporal organ, upon the volition of the animal. Of this lofty species of instinct the coral-worm affords a remarkable instance. This little creature, the architect of continents, is not only capable of building ramparts against the sea, with a precision of purpose, and scientific adaptation and arrangement, from which the most skillful engineer might imbibe his best knowledge — but is gifted of prophecy. It will foresee, for months in advance, the pure accidents which are to happen to its dwelling, and aided by myriads of its brethren, all acting as if with one mind (and *indeed* acting with only one — with the mind of the Creator) will work diligently to counteract influences which exist alone in the future. There is also an immensely wonderful consideration connected with the cell of the bee. Let a mathematician be required to solve the problem of the shape best calculated in such a cell as the bee wants, for the two requisites of strength and space — and he will find himself involved in the very highest and most abstruse questions of analytical research. Let him be required to tell the number of sides which will give to the cell the greatest space, with the greatest solidity, and to define the exact angle at which, with the same object in view, the roof must incline — and to answer the query, he must be a Newton or a Laplace. Yet since bees were, they have been continually solving the problem. The leading distinction between instinct and reason seems to be, that, while the one is infinitely the more exact, the more certain, and the more far-seeing in its sphere of action — the sphere of action in the other is of the far wider extent. But we are preaching a homily, when we merely intended to tell a short story about a cat.

The writer of this article is the owner of one of the most remarkable black cats in the world — and this saying much; for it will be remembered that black cats are all of them witches. The one in question has not a white hair about her, and is of a demure and sanctified demeanor. That portion of the kitchen which she most frequents is accessible only by a door, which closes with what is termed a thumb-latch; these latches are rude in construction, and some force and dexterity are always requisite to force them down. But puss is in the daily habit of opening the door, which she accomplished in the following way. She first springs from the ground to the guard of the latch (which resembles the guard over a gun-trigger,) and through this she thrusts her left arm to hold on with. She now, with her right hand, presses the thumb-latch until it yields, and here several attempts are frequently requisite. Having forced it down, however, she seems to be aware that her task is but half accomplished, since, if the door is not pushed open before she lets go, the latch will again fall into its socket. She, therefore, screws her body round so as to bring her hind feet immediately beneath the latch, while she leaps with all her strength from the door — the impetus of the spring forcing it open, and her hind feet sustaining the latch until this impetus is fairly given.

We have witnessed this singular feat a hundred times at least, and never without being impressed with the truth of the remark 75 with which we commenced this article — that the boundary between instinct and reason is of a very shadowy nature. The black cat, in doing what she did, must have made use of all the perceptive and reflective faculties which we are in the habit of supposing the prescriptive qualities of reason alone. 80

NOTES

1 ＊は主に Mobbott 版全集注釈を参照
2 下線は引用者による
3 *The Holy Bible: Authorized King James Version*
　　および『欽定訳聖書』1955 年改訳版を使用

THE BLACK CAT

　本作品には,「輪廻転生」,「天邪鬼根性」,「復讐劇」,「犯罪の必然的な露見」, といった当時のポーの心を捉えていたテーマがいくつも組み込まれている。主人公「私」の妻がいみじくも「黒猫＝魔女の化身」と口にしたように, 黒猫は悪魔のお気に入りの現身であるという中世の迷信に基づいたオカルト・ホラー。初出は *United Saturday Post* (1843 年 8 月 19 日付)。本テキストでは, Mabbott 版全集所収の *Tales* (1845 年)の原文を使用した。

　主人公「私」は, 優しく繊細だが, 意志が弱く, 動物だけが友達で, 悲劇続きで, 酒に溺れ, 可愛がっていた愛猫の目を抉った挙句その首を吊り, 最後には悪魔に憑かれたように妻を殺してしまう。

　発表当時から好評を博し, 翌年にはパロディが書かれるほどだった。タイトルの魅力も相俟って多くの映画が創られたが, ほとんどがタイトルを借用しただけで原作のプロットとはかけ離れたものばかりである。ロジャー・コーマン監督 (Roger Corman, 1926-)の『黒猫の怨霊』(*Tales of Terror* 1962 年)が, 最も原作に忠実である。なお日本では饗庭篁村 (1855-1922)の「黒猫」(1887 年[明治 20 年], 『読売新聞』)が本邦初のポー翻訳作品である。

2　FOR　→ nor solicit belief *for*
3　pen (v.) 書く
8　succinctly ＝ concisely
11　little but ＝ almost only
12　barroque(s) ここでは "bizarre" の意味, 奇異な, 奇怪な
23　caress (愛撫するように) 軽くなでる, (人を) 優しく扱う
45　Pluto ギリシャ神話のハデス(黄泉の国, 地獄)の王の名前, 冥王星

51 through the instrumentality of　～のせいで, ～にそそのかされて
instrumentality　尽力, 仲介

51 Intemperance (= alcoholism)　不摂生, アルコール依存症

71 gin [酒] 穀物や麦芽を原料として, Juniper berry(ヒノキ科ビャクシン
属の針葉樹である西洋ネズの果実を乾燥させたもの)で香りをつけた無
色透明の蒸留酒。カクテルベースとして用いられることも多い。19世
紀のアメリカでは安酒場でよく提供されていた。

74 socket　眼窩 (がんか)

90 perverseness　つむじ曲がり, 天邪鬼 (あまのじゃく)　cf.「天邪鬼」
(“The Imp of the Perverse” 1845 年)

91 * 初出の版では, ここに “Phrenology finds no place for it among its
organs.”という一文が挿入されている。

91 than I am that　=　than I am *sure* that

97 in the teeth of ～　=in spite of～　～にもかかわらず

104 in cool(cold) blood　冷酷に, 平然として　cf. ⇔ in hot (warm) blood
激怒して

110 jeopardize　危険にさらす　cf. double jeopardy

120 above　～というほどではない

127 plastering　漆喰

133 bas relief [フランス語] 浅浮き彫り

140 adjacent to ～　～の近く

146 lime　石灰

147 carcass　屍体, 残骸

150 it did not the less fail to ～　～しておかずにはいられなかった

154 went(go) so far as～　(こともあろうに)～するようにまでになった

159 infamy　醜聞, 非行, 不名誉　cf. Day of Infamy

162 rum [酒] 西インド諸島原産, サトウキビの廃糖蜜または絞り汁を原料
として作られる蒸留酒。カクテルベースとしても用いられる。航海の
ストレス緩和のために, 船内に常備されていたともいわれ, 海の男ある
いは海賊のイメージと結びついている。

199 partiality　偏愛 (for), 特別に好むこと

212 own　自白する, 罪を認容する

212 felon's cell　fellon　重罪犯／cell　刑務所の独房

215 chimera(s)　ギリシャ神話の怪物キメラ, 異種混交 (頭はライオン, 体
は山羊, 尾は蛇) の女怪物で火を吐く

222 at length　= at last

226 had I dared = if I had dared　できることなら

227 gallows　絞首台

228 engine　手段, 道具 [古]

233 * 旧約聖書「創世記」より "God created man in his own image."
(*Genesis* 1:27)「神は自分のかたちに人を創造された。」

246 abandon oneself to 〜　〜に身を任せる, 夢中になる

248 sufferer　苦しむ者, 受難者

261 set oneself forthwith to 〜　すぐさま〜にとりかかる

271 hit upon　ふと思いつく

279 false chimney　飾り煙突

285 crowbar　鉄梃, バール

288 hair　モルタルや砂と混ぜて「繋ぎ」として使用する毛のこと

291 * 実際にポーはボルティモアの煉瓦積み工事をした経験があったようだ。
cf.『アモンティリャードの酒樽』("The Cask of Amontillado" 1846 年)

311 premises　邸内, 屋敷

329 by way of 〜　〜のつもりで

341 * 旧約聖書「申命記」より "the wife of thy bosom" (*Deuteronomy*
13:6), "the wife of his bosom" (28:54)

350 damnation　地獄に落とす(落ちる)こと, 天罰

359 informing voice　告発する声

359 consign　引き渡す

SHADOW — A PARABLE

　「影」はポーの初期傑作の一つである。初出は *Southern Literary Messenger* (1835 年 1 月号), 後に『グロテスクとアラベスクの物語』(*The Tales of Grotesque and Arabesque* 1840 年) に収録された。本テキストでは *Tales* (1845 年) からの原文を使用。

　本作品は, King James 版の『聖書』を彷彿とさせる文体で書かれている。物語の舞台は古代ギリシャローマ文明の影響の残る黄昏時のエジプト。細部に至るまで歴史的背景に驚くほど忠実であるが,「死」や「生」といった普遍的なテーマを扱っているため, 歴史を学んでいない読者にとっても理解しやすいものになっている。

　本作執筆より少し前, 1831 年頃ボルティモアではコレラが流行り, 空には彗星が現れて不気味な霊気を放ち, 人々を恐怖に陥らせたといわれている。

疫病の時代を描いた作品は, 本作の他に「ペスト王」("King Pest" 1835 年),「赤き死の仮面劇」[後掲]等がある。

なお「影」という言葉はポーの作品では恐怖, 闇, 未知なるもの, 亡霊, 死, 等様々な意味を持つ。

1　parable　寓(ぐう)話, 教訓を含んだ短い物語, (主に聖書の)たとえ話, イエスによって語られた話の総称 cf. 新約聖書「マタイによる福音書」より "All these things spake Jesus unto the multitude in parables; and without a parable spake he not unto them" (*Matthew* 13:34)「イエスはこれらのことをすべて, 譬(たとえ)で群衆に語られた。譬によらないでは何事も彼らに語られなかった。」

2　Yea! though I walk through the valley of the *Shadow:* ——*Psalm of David*「たとえわれ死の影を歩むとも——ダビデ詩篇」cf. 旧約聖書「詩篇」より "Yea, though I walk through the valley of the shadow of death, I will fear no evil: for thou art with me; thy rod and thy staff they comfort me."(*Psalm* 23:4)「たといわたしは死の影の谷を歩むとも, 私はわざわいを恐れません。あなたがわたしと共におられるからです。あなたのむちと, あなたのつえはわたしを慰めます。」

　　大岡昇平は『野火』(1951 年)のエピグラフにこの句を引用しているが, 本作から借用したと語っている。

7　ere　～する前に, ～しないうちに

7　be seen of men　新約聖書「マタイによる福音書」より　cf. "And when thou prayest, thou shalt not be as the hypocrites *are*: for they love to pray standing in the synagogues and in the corners of the streets, that they may be seen of men. Verily I say unto you, They have their reward."(*Matthew* 6:5)「また祈る時には, 偽善者たちのようにするな。彼らは, 人に見せようとして, 会堂や大通りのつじに立って祈ることを好む。よく言っておくが, 彼らはその報いを受けてしまっている。」

10　chracter(s)　文字

10　with a stylus of iron　鉄の尖筆で　cf. "a pen of iron"は新約聖書「エレミヤ書」に, "an iron pen"は旧約聖書「ヨブ記」に記述がある。"The sin of Judah *is* written with a pen of iron, *and* with the point of a diamond: *it is* graven upon the table of their heart, and upon the horns of your altars;"(*Jeremiah* 17:1)「ユダの罪は, 鉄の筆, 金剛石のとがりをもってしるされ, 彼らの心の碑と, 祭壇の角に彫りつ

けられている。」／ "That they were graven with an iron pen and lead in the rock for ever!"(*Job* 19: 24) 「鉄の筆と鉛とをもって，ながく岩に刻みつけられるように。」

　　ポーは『スタイラス』(*The Stylus*)という雑誌の創刊を企画していた。

14 * 紀元前 542 年頃，ユスティニアヌス 1 世(東ローマ帝国)の治世下，ナイル川の三角州地帯で最も東側の河口に位置した古代エジプトの町ペルシウムの港で，最初に疫病が発生したとみられている。

15 cunning 〜に優れた，熟練の

17 Oinos オイノス[人名], [ギリシャ語] "one", "individual"の意味

19 Aries 白羊宮，牡羊座

19 Jupitar 木星

20 Saturnus 土星

24 Chian wine ヒオス島(Chios)産のワイン，ヒオス島(キオス島とも表記される)はエーゲ海東部に位置する現ギリシャ領の島

25 Ptolemais プトレマイス[地名]リビア北東部，キレナイカ地方にある古代ギリシャの都市。古代エジプトのプトレマイオス三世にちなんで名づけられ，紀元前 6 世紀に建設，4 世紀から 3 世紀にかけて商業港として繁栄した。

28 * "Corinnos"は，トロイ戦争の頃の伝説的な詩人の名前であり，当時の記録にこの名を持つ「名工」の名前はない。おそらく，当時金属細工で有名だった芸術の中心地，ギリシャ南部の海港コリントス(Corinth)出身の者ということを，ポーは示唆しているのだろう。

36 The nervous ＝ nervous people

49 Anacreon アナクレオン[人名] 愛とワインを讃えた詩で有名な古代ギリシャの詩人 cf. 米英戦争(War of 1812, 1812-1815)のさなかに弁護士でアマチュア詩人の F・スコット・キー(Francis Scott Key, 1779-1843)が書いた詩 "Defence of Fort McHenry"に，イギリスの作曲家ジョン・S・スミス(1750-1836) が作り，当時英米で人気を博していた "To Anacreon in Heaven"のメロディーを付したものが，アメリカ国歌 "The Star-Spangled Banner"の原型である。

52 Zoilus ゾイラス[人名] 「生命」を意味する "zoë"に由来する。

63 Teios テオス[地名] 現トルコ領のアナトリア半島西部にあったイオニア地方の港町。アナクレオンは紀元前 550 年頃にここで生まれ，「テオスの息子」あるいは「テオスの男」と呼ばれていた。

75 Chaldea カルデア[地名] ユーフラテス・デルタとペルシャ湾とアラビア砂漠の間に位置するメソポタミア南部の古代地域

79 over against 〜に面して, 〜の真向かいに

87 the Catacombs 地下墓地, 古代ローマではキリスト教徒の避難所となっていた。

87 hard by すぐ近くに

88 Charonian カロン(Charon)の, カロンはギリシャ神話における三途の川ステュクス河で, 死者の魂を黄泉の国(Hades)に運ぶ渡し守のこと

93 fall upon our ears 耳に聞こえてくる

THE MASQUE OF THE RED DEATH

　「赤き死の仮面劇」は *Graham's Magazine* (1842年5月)から発表されたゴシック・ロマンスの代表的作品である。タイトルは *Broadway Journal* (1845年7月)に掲載される際に「仮面」("mask")から「仮面劇」("masque")へと変更されたが, それ以外は目立った改稿はほとんどなされていないほど, 当初から完璧な作品として出版された。本テキストでは *Tales*(1845年)の原文を使用。オマージュ作品も多く書かれているが, 中でもアメリカの幻想怪奇小説家 H・P・ラヴクラフト(Howard Phillips Lovecraft, 1890-1937)の「アウトサイダー」("The Outsider" 1921年)は, 本作品と対にして楽しめる傑作である。一貫して侵入者側の視点から作品は描かれており, 侵入の経緯, 方法, そしてその理由まで明かされる。

　「赤き死」("Red Death")は, 1831年のボルティモアでのコレラの流行や妻ヴァージニアの喀血などに着想を得た創作上の疫病であるが, 作品自体はイタリアの散文家ボッカッチョ(Giovanni Boccaccio, 1313-1375)の『デカメロン』(*Decameron* 1348-1353年)の設定を想起させる。また文学的なインスピレーションとして, シェイクスピアの戯曲から2つのソースが指摘されている。『嵐』(1612年)での奴隷キャリバンの台詞 "You taught me language; and my profit on't／Is, I know how to curse／The red plague rid you／For learning me your language!"(*Tempest*, I. 2. 363-64)と, 『コリオレイナス』(1607年)の "Now the red pestilence strike all trades in Rome,／And occupations perish!"(*Coriolanus*, IV. 1. 13)である。また近年では, 本作品より百年以上後の1976年にスーダン南西部で発見されたエボラウイルスとの近似性も注目に値するとの指摘がある。

　3 ＊旧約聖書「出エジプト記」より "Take thy rod, and stretch out thine hand upon the waters of Egypt... that they may become blood... and all the waters that *were* in the river were turned to <u>blood</u>... and there was <u>blood</u> throughout all the land of Egypt." (*Exodus* 7:19-21)

4 Avatar　ヒンドゥー教神話の神(ヴィシュヌ神)の化身。ヴィシュヌ神は，三神一体の最高神で，繁栄あるいは世界の維持を司る役割を持つ。

6 scarlet　緋色，深紅色，罪悪(時に性的な)を象徴する。cf. scarlet crime, ナサニエル・ホーソーン『緋文字』(Nathaniel Hawthorne *The Scarlet Letter* 1850 年)

8 ban　禁止令，布告

21 ingress or egress　出入口

26 buffoon　道化

26 improvisatori [イタリア語・複] 即興詩人　cf. improvisatore [単]

27 * 初出の版には，この後に "there were cards," という一文がある。

33 ball　舞踏会

36 suite　一続きの部屋

40 bizarre [フランス語] 奇怪な，異様な ＝ fantastic, grotesque

42 little more than ～　せいぜい～に過ぎない

45 look out upon ～　～に面する，臨む

61 candelabrum (複数の灯が立てられる)装飾の施された枝付き燭台

79 lung　肺，ここでは時計を擬人化している。

83 harken to ＝ hearken to　耳を傾ける

84 * 1842 年当時，ワルツは猥褻な感じのするものとみなされていた。

100 decora [ラテン語・複] 気品，身だしなみ，秩序正しさ　cf. decorum [単]

106 fête [フランス語] ＝ feast 饗宴(きようえん)

110 * 1830 年パリで初演のフランスの作家ヴィクトル・ユーゴー(Victor Hugo, 1802-1885)作の五幕韻文劇『エルナニ』(*Hernani, ou l'Honneur Castillan*)のこと。16 世紀のスペインを舞台に，貴族の娘ドニャ・ソルをめぐって元貴族で山賊のエルナニと王カルロス，老公爵リュイ・ゴメスが絡みあう。最後はエルナニ，ゴメス，ソル皆悲劇の死を遂げる。ロマン派宣言の実践とされる作品で，古典演劇派の形式を打破し，ロマン主義演劇の先駆けとなった(エルナニ事件)。1844 年にヴェニスで初演のイタリアのロマン派作曲家ヴェルディ (Giuseppe Fortunino Francesco Verdi, 1813-1901)の四幕オペラ『エルナーニ』(*Ernani*)はこの作品に着想を得ている。ヴェルディ初期作品の傑作の一つである。

119 anon　そのうち，直ちに [古]

157 * out-Heroded Herod　ヘロデ王をも凌ぐほど残虐で放縦な　cf. ヘロ

デ王はその残虐さで有名なユダヤの王で, イエス・キリストを殺害する
ためベツレヘムの男の幼児の皆殺しを命じた王として知られる。新約
聖書「マタイによる福音書」より "Then Herod, when he saw that he
was mocked of the wise men, was exceeding wroth, and sent
forth, and slew all the children that were in Bethlehem, and in
all the coasts thereof, from two years old and under, according
to the time which he had diligently enquired of the wise men."
(*Matthew* 2:16) なお『ハムレット』(1603 年)には "it out-herods Herod:
pray you, avoid it."(*Hamlet*, III. 2. 16) という表現があり, ポーはこれを
気に入っており「メッツェンガースタイン」("Metzengerstein" 1832 年),
「ウィリアム・ウィルソン」("William Wilson" 1839 年)でも使用している。

166 habiliment of the grave 死装束

170 mummer 無言劇の役者

197 person = body, 身体

224 * 新約聖書「テサロニケ人への第一の手紙」より "For yourselves know
perfectly that the day of the Lord so cometh as a thief in the night."
(*I Thessalonians* 5:2)「あなたがた自身がよく知っているとおり, 主の
日は盗人が夜くるように来る。」

DEVIL IN THE BELFRY

　当時増大しつつあったアイルランド移民人口の問題や経済成長に伴う時
計の普及などが, 風刺としてとりあげられている。初出は *The Saturday
Chronicle*(1839 年 3 月 8 日付)。原文は, 編集者でポーの遺稿管理人であった
ルーファス・W・グリズウォルド(Rufus Wilmot Griswold, 1815-1857)が
編集した *The Works of the Late Edgar Allan Poe* (1850)より。

　時計を象って形成されている閉鎖的な一つの町が, 楽器を抱えた得体の
知れない男の登場によって, 時間の流れを狂わされて秩序を失ってしまう
という奇譚。ヴァンダーヴォッテイミティス(wonder what time it is)と
いう「旧き秩序」を重んじる保守的な町に, 丘の向こうから, 奇妙な楽器を
抱えた異国風の男が, 軽やかにステップを踏みながらやってくる。この男
は町の象徴である鐘楼の大時計を乗っ取り, 鐘を我が物顔に鳴らしながら,
これみよがしにアイルランド民謡を奏でてみせる。

　作品自体が音楽的効果を意識して創作されており,「アッシャー館の崩
壊」("The Fall of the House of Usher" 1839 年)と同様に, フランスの作曲

家クロード・ドビュッシー(Claude Achille Debussy, 1862-1918)がオペラ化しようと試みている(青柳いづみこ『ドビュッシー 想念のエクトプラズム』中公文庫, 2008 年／池末陽子「「鐘楼の悪魔」における音風景——ポー, 悪魔, そしてハープ」『悪魔とハープ——エドガー・アラン・ポーと十九世紀アメリカ』音羽書房鶴見書店, 2008 年)。近年では F・コッポラ監督(Francis Ford Coppola, 1939-)の映画『Virginia/ヴァージニア』(*Twixt*, 2011 年) に, 複数面の時計台のモチーフが使われている。また森鴎外翻訳の「十三時」はポーの英語原文からではなく, ドイツ語訳から邦訳したものである。

1 * 初出のタイトルには, "An Extravaganza" という副題が付されていた。「奇矯な言行」を意味する。なおエクストラヴァガンザは, ヴィクトリア朝文芸の影響を受けて 19 世紀アメリカで流行した, 奇抜で自由な様式や構造の文学, 劇, 音楽やミュージカルを指す。

2 *old saying* 古諺(こげん), 古い言い伝え

4 Dutch borough オランダの町; borough は自治町村あるいは行政区のこと(アメリカ)。* 作品の中では, おそらく Pennsylvania Dutch のこと, つまりペンシルバニア州東部のドイツ系移民居留地を指すのだが, 本作に描かれる人々の姿はニューヨークのオランダ移民居留地の人々とよく似ている。また一説によれば, この作品の風景は, ポーの養父ジョン・アランの故郷であるスコットランドのエアシャー(Ayrshire)のイメージを髣髴とさせる。ポーは少年の頃, 家族とともにこの地を訪れている。

4 Vondervotteimittiss = "[I] wonder what time it is."

16 authority 権威, 信頼や裏付けがある知識や情報, あるいはそれらを与えてくれる人や書物

24 algebraic formula 代数式

37 the Town Council 議会議事堂, あるいは議員一同

38 commit myself on〜 〜について意見を述べる, 去就を明らかにする

39 *Oratiuncitlæ de Rebus Præter-Veteris* [ラテン語] = *A Brief Thesis on Things Extraordinary Old*

41 Folio 二折判, 左右見開き両頁

42 Catch-word 見出し語

42 Cypher 頁数

66 picturesque 18 世紀末頃のイギリスで興隆した, 田園風景や異国趣味などの絵画的な雰囲気を尊重する美的概念。主に庭園美学で用いられ始めた概念で, 絵のように美しい, 描写や表現が生き生きして真に迫っ

ていることを表す。

67 with black ends 両端が黒い

69 gable 破風 (はふ), 勾配屋根に造られる三角形の外壁部分

69 cornice コーニス, 古代ギリシャ・ローマ建築で, entablature (柱で支えられる水平材) の最上部をなす突出部

88 China man 陶磁器の人形

93 sauer-kraut 塩漬けキャベツ

96 sugar-loaf 円錐形の砂糖菓子

106 repeater ＝ a toy watch, 時報時計, 同じ物事を繰り返す人やものの総称

112 surtout シュルトゥ, 19世紀に流行した男子用のぴったりしたオーバーコート

135 oily 脂性の, 口先のうまい

136 saucer 皿のような, 丸い

144 stick by〜 〜を守る, 忠実である

163 clapper 鐘の舌

165 burgher(s) 住民

168 offices 職務, 任務

193 finnicky (finicky) 凝り性の

199 do up 手入れをする, お粧(め)かしをする

200 papillotes パピヨット, 巻き紙, 料理で使う油紙

203 pumps 舞踏靴

204 for bows 蝶結びにして

204 chapeau-de-bras 折りたたんで脇に挟むことができる三角帽子。後にアメリカでは, 軍隊で使用された(chapeau-bras)。

205 fiddle 弓を用いる擦弦楽器で, ヴァイオリンと全く同じ構造を持つ。多様な民俗音楽の伝統や背景があり, 19世紀のアメリカでは街辻などでアイルランド人が楽器演奏するのがよくみられた。

212 curvet 跳ね回る(クルベット, 前足が着地する前に後ろ脚だけで軽く跳躍前進させる高等な馬術)

216 cambric 薄地の白い麻布

218 popinjay 粧(め)かし屋, 洒落(しゃれ)た人

219 fandango ファンダンゴ, 特殊アクセントを伴う3拍子の民族舞曲

219 whirligig 旋回, 回転運動

220 keeping time 「拍子をとる」と「時間を守る」の2つの意味に用いられている。

225 chassez 片方の足で常にリードしながら速く滑るように進むステップ

225 balancez 3拍子の曲に合わせて, 前後左右に揺れるように動くステップ

226 pirouette 片方のつま先で旋回するステップ

226 pas-de-zéphyr 片足で立って, もう片方の足を振るステップ cf.「息の喪失」("Loss of Breath" 1832 年)

235 * Devil's tattoo いらいらと指先で机などをコツコツ叩く

248 "Von" 「1」のこと cf. ここから先 1〜13 の数詞らしき単語が並ぶが, これらは単に英語を崩して, オランダ語かドイツ語らしく見せかけているだけである。

264 Der Teufel! [ドイツ語] = The Devil! なんてこった

267 Mein Gott [ドイツ語] = My God なんてことだ, 大変だ

268 * 時計が 13 時を知らせるのは,「死の予兆」や「運が悪いこと」であると解釈される。

271 "Vot is cum'd to mein pelly? = What has become of my berry? "cum'd"は "come" (の過去分詞のつもり), "pelly"は "berry"のこと

276 Donder and Blitzen! 畜生め！

281 old Nick 悪魔, * 北海の神の直系子孫

283 take to〜 〜に熱中する, 没頭する

284 contain themselves(oneself) 気持ちを抑える, 自制する

303 "Judy O'Flannagan" and "Paddy O'Raferty" 古いアイルランド民謡, "Paddy"はアイルランド人を(ふざけて軽蔑的に)指す。

A TALE OF THE RAGGED MOUNTAINS

　語り手の友人ベドロー氏は鋸山散策中に不思議な光景に出会う。ポー作品にお馴染みのテーマ「催眠術」と「輪廻転生」を主軸にしたオカルトファンタジー。初出は *Godey's Magazine and Lady's Book*(1844 年 4 月号)。本テキストで使用している原文は, 翌年の *Broadway Journal* (1845 年 11 月 29 日付)に再掲されたもの。

　「鋸山奇譚」の舞台となっているシャーロッツヴィルと「鋸山」の描写は, ポー自身の体験を描いたものとみられる。鋸山は標高 1000 フィート、リンチバーグに至るハイウェイ近くのシャーロッツヴィルの南西に位置する 80 マイル四方の場所である。

　2 Charlottesville [地名] シャーロッツヴィル, ヴァージニア州中央部に

ある都市。第3代大統領トマス・ジェファソン(Thomas Jefferson, 1743-1826)が設立したヴァージニア大学(University of Virginia)があり，ポーは退学するまでここに通った。

8　Whence　どこから

25　feline　ネコ科の

40　physician　医師 (特に内科医)

42　* Saratoga Springs　サラトガ・スプリングはニューヨーク州サラトガ郡にある都市。植民地時代から，療法上効能のある鉱泉として有名で，1820年には人気の保養地となっていた。ポーはこの地を1843年の夏に訪れ，詩「大鴉」(後掲)を執筆したといわれている。

48　invalid　患者，病人

51　* フランツ・アントン・メスメル(Franz Anton Mesmer, 1733-1815) 磁気催眠療法で有名なドイツの内科医。メスメリズム (mesmerism)とは，人体は動物磁気(宇宙に遍在する磁気的性質を帯びた微細な粒子からなる流体)の作用下にあり，磁気の不均衡が生じると病気になるという説

64　rapport　交感，心が通い合っていること

73　volition　意志作用，決断力

77　* cf.「催眠術の啓示」("Mesmeric Revelation" 1844年)，「ヴァルドマアル氏の病症の真相」("The Facts in the Case of M. Valdemar" 1845年)

81　morphine　モルヒネ，ケシを原料とする鎮痛剤。1805年頃，精神催眠薬として使用された。1853年注射による投与が可能になり，南北戦争 (1861-1865)で盛んに使用された。中毒性がある。薬名はギリシャ神話の夢神モルペウス(Morpheus)にちなんでつけられた。

91　interregnum　空白期間，合い間

116　Indian Summer　小春日和，アメリカ北部の10月から11月にかけて続く異常に温暖な日のこと。一般によく晴れてはいるが，煙霧がかかったようになり，夜間はかなり冷え込む。

125　trefoil　シロツメクサ，三つ葉模様の

128　rhapsodical (rhapsodic)　狂想的な

143　Archangel　大天使，天使長　* 新約聖書「テサロニケ人への第1の手紙」より "For the Lord... shall descend from heaven with a shout, with the voice of the archangel, and with the trump."(*I Thessalonians* 4:16)「すなわち，主ご自身が天使のかしらの声と神のラッパが鳴り響くうちに，合図の声で天から下ってこられる。」

153 hyena ハイエナ, 死肉を食す夜行性のイヌに似た動物。アフリカ, インド, 中東, ネパール南部に分布し, 主にサバンナや低木林に生息する。貪欲の象徴とされ, 吠え声は悪魔の笑い声に例えられる。

169 palm ヤシ, 汎熱帯植物でヤシ科の高木の総称

181 enchanter 魔法使い

193 minaret ミナレット, (イスラム教寺院の)光塔

193 shrine 聖堂, 廟(びょう), 日本の神社

205 mosque モスク, イスラム教寺院 * ベナレス(バラナシ, ヒンドゥー教最大の聖地)のモスクは, 北インドのムガル帝国(トルコ系イスラム王朝 1526-1858)の第六代君主アウラングゼーブ(Aurungzeb 統治期間 1678-1707)によって建てられた。

225 Novalis ノヴァーリス [筆名] (本名 Georg Philipp Friedrich von Hardenberg, 1772-1801) ドイツ・ロマン主義の詩人, 小説家, 思想家

251 kiosk (トルコの)あずまや, 庭園などにある簡易建築物

271 creese 波形の刃付きのマレー半島の短剣

301 galvanic battery 1790 年頃イタリアの生理学者ガルバーニ(Luigi Galvani, 1737-1798)によって動物電気の理論が提唱され, 1800 年物理学者ボルタ(Count Alessandro Volta, 1745-1827)によって電池が発明された。* cf.「息の喪失」[前掲]

324 Calcutta カルカッタ, インド北東部, 西ベンガル州南東部にある同州の州都。ガンジス川の三角州分流フーグリ川の東岸, 河口から約 130km に位置する。1690 年よりイギリスのインド支配の拠点であり, 1772 年から 1911 年(デリー遷都)まで首都とされた。2001 年より「コルカタ」(ベンガル語)に正式名称が変更された。

336 the Holy River 聖河, ガンジス川のこと

338 * チェイテ・シン(当時のベナレスの藩王=Rajah)の叛乱, 英国領インド初代総督ウォーレン・ヘイスティング(Warren Hastings, 1732-1818)の重税政策に耐えかねて蜂起した。本文では暴動は「1780 年」に起こったとなっているが, ヘイスティングスの手記によれば「1781 年」である。

341 sepoy 元英領インド軍のインド人傭兵

356 neuralgia 神経痛

366 venomous 有毒な, 毒液を分泌する

366 sangsue サングスー, 蛭(ひる)の一種, *フランス語から借用したポーの創作上の生物

368 artery 静脈

382 typographical error 誤植, 誤脱

THE RAVEN

　各スタンザの末尾に繰り返される "Nevermore" の語りで有名な物語詩。第四詩集である『大鴉とその他の詩』(*The Raven and Other Poems* 1845年)に収録。初出は *Evening Mirror*(1845年1月29日版)。発表後数週間のうちに次々に紙面に再掲載され、パロディーも出回るほど好評を博し、「大鴉」はポーのニックネームともなった。翌1846年「詩作の哲学」("The Philosophy of Composition")の中で、ポー自身がこの詩の意図、創作過程、詩体について、(多分に虚構的ではあるが)詳細な分析をおこなっている。原文はポー生前に *Semi-Weekly Examiner* に発表された最終版。なお2012年には、同タイトルの映画がジョン・キューザック主演で公開されている(邦題は『推理作家ポー 最期の5日間』)。

　ポーの詩の特徴は、音楽性と物語性が際立っていることにある。リズムや韻が重視され、響きの美しさを最大限に引き出す言葉が散りばめられている。「大鴉」は各6行の18スタンザで構成され、韻律は強弱八歩格(trochaic octameter)であるが、ポーは次のように語っている。

　" Of course, I pretend to no originality in either the rhythm or metre of the "Raven." The former is trochaic — the latter is octametre acatalectic, alternating with heptameter catalectic repeated in the refrain of the fifth verse, and terminating with tetrameter catalectic. Less pedantically — the feet employed throughout (trochees) consist of a long syllable followed by a short: the first line of the stanza consists of eight of these feet — the second of seven and a half (in effect two-thirds) — the third of eight — the fourth of seven and a half — the fifth the same — the sixth three and a half. Now, each of these lines, taken individually, has been employed before, and what originality the "Raven" has, is in their combination into stanza; nothing even remotely approaching this combination has ever been attempted. The effect of this originality of combination is aided by other unusual, and some altogether novel effects, arising from an extension of the application of the principles of rhyme and alliteration." 「もちろんわたしは「鴉」が韻律においても歩格においても独創的であるというつもりはない。前者は強弱格——後者は完全八歩格であって、第五行のリフレインで繰り返される不完全七歩格と交代し、不完全四歩格で終わる。もっと簡単に言えば——全体を通じ

て用いられている詩脚(強弱格)は一個の長音節とそれに続く一個の単音節からなっている。連の第一行はこういう八個の詩脚からなり、第二行は七個半(実際には三分の二)、第三行は八個、第四行は七個半、第五行も同じ、第六行は三個半である。ところで、こういう行を個々に見てみれば、みな以前に用いられたものばかりであって、そうなると「鴉」の独創性はそれらを組み合わせて連にしたところにあるだけだが、こういう組み合わせにすこしでも似た試みがなされたことは、いまだかつてなかったのである。この組み合せの独創性の効果は、踏韻と頭韻の原理を拡大適用することから生じた予想外の斬新な効果によって補強された。」(八木敏雄訳『ポオ評論集』岩波書店, 2009 年)

1 Raven 大鴉, 普通の crow よりは大きく全長約 60cm。北半球の高緯度地域に生息するワタリガラスの一種。疫病や死など凶兆の予知をするといわれる。ポーは「詩作の哲学」で "the bird of ill omen" と呼んでいる。cf. ポーの詩や小説の中の大鴉や黒猫は, 自然から脅威と恐怖を引き出す「エコ恐怖(ecophobia)」が形成する自然表象であるゴシック・ネイチャーとして論じることができる(伊藤詔子『ディズマル・スワンプのアメリカン・ルネッサンス——ポーとダークキャノン』音羽書房鶴見書店, 2017 年)。

2 *「大鴉」の冒頭は, ポーが好んだアイルランドの詩人トマス・ムーア (Thomas Moore, 1779-1852)による翻訳詩集『アナクレオンの頌歌』(*Anacreaontea* 1800 年)の作品 33 に近似している。

2 *「ライジーア」("Ligeia" 1838 年)のヒロインの髪は, "raven-like" や "it was blacker than the raven wings of the midnight!" と表現されている。

8 キリスト教歴において 12 月はもっとも暗黒の力が増す時期とされる。

11 Lenore 若くして亡くなった恋人の名前 cf. "Lenore"(1831 年)

37 *wind シェイクスピアの『オセロ』(1602 年)に, オセロの妻でデズデモーナの問いに, イアーゴーの妻エミリアが答える次のような台詞がある。
"Hark! who is't that Knocks? —— It's the wind."(*Othello*, I. 3. 53)

42 Pallas パラス[人名]; パラス・アテーナーのこと。ギリシャ神話のオリュンポス十二神の一柱で, 知恵, 芸術, 戦略を司るアテネの守護女神。梟(ふくろう)を聖鳥とする。

46 craven 臆病な, 敗北した [古]

48 Plutonian 黄泉の国の cf. Pluto ("The Black Cat")

66 dirge 葬送歌, 哀歌

81 censer 香炉, 宗教儀式の際には鎖の吊り手を振って用いる。

82 seraphim 天使 cf. seraph [単]

85 nepenthe ネペンテス, 憂いや悲しみ, 苦痛を忘れさせてくれる抗鬱薬, 古代ギリシャ人が使ったとされる忘れ薬のこと

86 Quaff 飲むがよい

92 balm in Gilead ギレアドバルサムノキから採った芳香のある軟膏, 傷を癒す効能がある薬 * cf. Gilead ヨルダン東山岳地帯, 旧約聖書「創世記」より "a company of Ishmeelites came from Gilead with their camels bearing spicery and balm and myrrh, going to carry *it* down to Egypt."(*Genesis* 37:25)「イシマエルびとの隊商が, らくだに香料と, 乳香と, もつやくとを負わせてエジプトへ下り行こうとギレアデからやってきた。」／旧約聖書「エレミヤ書」より "Is there no balm in Gilead; *is there* no physician there? why then is not the health of the daughter of my people recovered?"(*Jeremiah* 8:22)「ギリアデには乳香があるではないか。そのところに医者がいるではないか。それにどうしてわが民の娘はいやされることがないのか。」

96 Aidenn = Eden エデンの園, 旧約聖書で人類の始祖アダム(Adam)とイヴ(Eve)が住んでいた楽園, * "heaven"を意味する。彼らが善悪を知る木の実を食べたとき, 二人は原罪(original sin)を犯したとして楽園を追放された。cf.「エロスとチャーミオンの対話」("The Conversation of Eros and Charmion" 1839 年),「言葉の力」("The Power of Words" 1845 年)

INSTINCT VS REASON — A BLACK CAT

　ポー自身幼い頃から猫が好きで, 黒猫を二代に渡って飼っていた。妻ヴァージニアは寒いときには猫を抱えて暖を採っていたという逸話が残っている。彼は短編小説「黒猫」[前掲]発表に先だって, 短いエッセイ「本能 vs. 理性――黒い猫について」を *Alexander's Weekly Messenger* (1840 年 1 月 29 日付)に掲載した。執筆時期から推測するに, この作品で描かれている猫は,「黒猫」の Pluto に容姿が似ていた二代目の Caterina (1844 年から 1849 年まで飼っていたらしい)のことではなく, 一代目の猫のことであろう。なおポーは, 動物界における非論理的な行動と思われる事柄について, かなり関心があったらしく, 幾つかの詩にもこのテーマを取り上げている("Romance" 1829 年, "Raven"[前掲]など)。

2 demarcate 限界を定める

5 settle 決着をつける

5 * "the North-Eastern"はメイン州と当時のイギリス領ニューブランズウィックの境界をめぐる紛争(アルーストック戦争)を指す。1842年ウェブスター・アッシュバートン条約をもって決着した。スペリオル湖とウッズ湖の間の境界の決定, 東海岸から西はロッキー山脈までの境界線は北緯49度線上あることの再確認などが, 条約の主な内容である。一方, "the Oregon" は オレゴン国境紛争のことを指す。イギリスが「コロンビア」と呼び, アメリカが「オレゴン」と呼んでいた, ロッキー山脈の西から太平洋までの北米西部の地域の領有権をめぐる争いは, 1846年のオレゴン条約で, 北緯49度線を境界線とすることで決着した。

7 reason 論理的に考える

9 reflective 思慮深い

11 perpetually 永久に

15 so far from being 〜 〜であるどころか

15 * exacted おそらく "exalted"の誤植である。

16 divine 神の恩恵を受けた

18 * lion-ant 蟻地獄(ant-lion) cf.『ジュリアス・ロドマンの日誌』(*The Journal of Julius Rodman* 1840年)

19 analogy 類推, 相似

22 Deity 神

23 corporal 身体の

27 adaptation 適応, 小説や戯曲などの脚色・翻案のこと

28 imbibe 取り入れる

31 myriad of 〜 〜無数の

31 brethren 仲間

38 requisite 必要条件

39 abstruse 難解な

48 far-seeing 先見の明がある

50 homily (長々しい)お説教

56 demure 上品ぶった

60 puss 猫(にゃんこ)ちゃん

72 impetus 勢い

74 feat 芸当

APPENDIX

テクスト

Levine Stuart and Susan, ed., *The Short Fiction of Edgar Allan Poe. An Annotated Edition.* University of Illinois Press, 1976.

Mabbott, Thomas Olive, ed. *Edgar Allan Poe: Tales and Sketches.* 2 vols. University of Illinois Press, 2000.

Pollin, Burton R., ed. *Collected Writings of Edgar Allan Poe.* 5 vols. Gordian, 1985-97.

Ostrom, John Ward, ed. *The Letter of Edgar Allan Poe.* 2 vols. Gordian, 1966.

Thompson J. R. *Edgar Allan Poe: Essays and Reviews.* Library of America, 1984.

参考翻訳

『E・A・ポー』鴻巣友季子・桜庭一樹編, 池末陽子 (編集協力) ＜ポケットマスターピース 09 (集英社文庫ヘリテージシリーズ)＞ 集英社, 2016 年

『黒猫・アッシャー家の崩壊』＜ポー短編集 I ゴシック編＞巽孝之訳, 新潮社, 2009 年

『黒猫／モルグ街の殺人』(光文社古典新訳文庫)小川高義訳, 光文社, 2006 年

伝記的資料

Quinn, A. H. *Edgar Allan Poe: A Critical Biography.* Johns Hopkins University Press, 1997.

Silverman, Kenneth. *Edgar Allan Poe: Mournful and Never-Ending Remembrance.* Harper, 1991.

Thomas, Dwight and David K. Jackson. *The Poe Log: A Documentary Life of Edgar Allan Poe 1809-1849.* G. K. Hall & Co., 1987.

辞典・必携参考文献

Frank, Frederick S. and Tony Magistrale. *The Poe Encyclopedia.* Greenwood, 1997.

Kennedy, J. Gerald and Scott Peeples. *The Oxford Handbook of Edgar Allan Poe.* Oxford University Press, 2019.

Sova, Dawn B. *Edgar Allan Poe A to Z: The Essential Reference to His Life and Work.* Facts on File, 2001.

巽孝之・八木敏雄編『エドガー・アラン・ポーの世紀 ＜生誕 200 周年記念必携＞』研究社, 2009 年

宮永孝『ポーと日本──その受容の歴史』彩流社, 2000 年

Selected Works of Edgar Allan Poe

E・A・ポー選集

©2019 年 9 月 4 日　　初版発行
2021 年 9 月 28 日　第 3 刷発行

編註者　　　　　　　　　池末陽子
発行者　　　　　　　　　原雅久
発行所　　　　　　　株式会社 朝日出版社
　　　〒101-0065　東京都千代田区西神田 3-3-5
　　　　　　　　☎　03-3239-0271/72
　　　　　　　　FAX　03-3239-0479
　　　　　e-mail text-e@asahipress.com
　　　　　　　振替口座 00140-2-46008
　　　　　　　　印刷・錦明印刷

ISBN978-4-255-15658-3 C1082